GREAT   HYMNS

and

THEIR   STORIES

# GREAT HYMNS

*and*

# THEIR STORIES

by

## W. J. LIMMER SHEPPARD

*O Lord and Master of us all,*
*Whate'er our name or sign,*
*We own Thy sway, we hear Thy Call,*
*We test our lives by Thine.*

*Yet weak and blinded though we be,*
*Thou dost our service own;*
*We bring our varying gifts to Thee.*
*And Thou rejectest none.*

J. G. WHITTIER

LUTTERWORTH PRESS

GUILDFORD AND LONDON

ALL RIGHTS RESERVED
*First published*      *1923*
*New edition*      *1950*
*First paperback edition*    *1979*

ISBN 0 7188 2451 2

*Printed in U.S.A.*

To

EUGENE STOCK, D.C.L.

*Without whose generous and practical appreciation the Author would probably never have become a Hymn-writer this volume is gratefully dedicated*

## Preface

THE contents of the following pages first appeared in a weekly paper, and with the generous and courteous permission of the Editor, this volume is now issued. Published in this more permanent form, I venture to hope that these Hymn Stories may be of lasting interest to a wide circle of readers. There are numerous volumes of Hymn Sermons already published, but the accounts of the way in which the hymns came into being are few and far between, so that these pages may supply a real need. The use of the word " great " in the title is not meant to imply literary greatness, but rather the influence of the hymn on audiences and individuals. The instances given of spiritual blessing resulting from hymns are merely a few examples; they could have been multiplied almost indefinitely had space permitted.

The main source of information in writing these stories has been, of course, Dr. Julian's monumental work, *The Dictionary of Hymnology.* Mr. Ira D. Sankey's volume, *My Life and Sacred Songs,* the Rev. G. R. Balleine's splendid *Lessons from the Hymn Book,* and Mr. G. J. Stevenson's *The Methodist Hymn Book* have furnished much interesting material.

I am thankful to know that, in their previous publication, these Hymn Stories have proved to be a spiritual help, and I trust that in this new form they will bring still further blessing to their readers, and greater glory to the Master.

W. J. LIMMER SHEPPARD.

## Contents

# Chapter 1

## *Thanksgiving for Peace*

During the Thirty Years' War (1620 to 1648) the little town of Eilenburg, in Saxony, suffered severely. The Austrians sacked it once and the Swedes twice. The overcrowding caused by the influx of refugees from the countryside produced the plague, which ravaged the city four times during the period of war. Only one minister of the town, Martin Rinkart, survived this scourge and it often fell to his lot to take as many as fifty funerals in a single day! Famine was yet another of the miseries of war which left its mark on Eilenburg, while of its thousand houses nearly eight hundred were laid in ruins.

But at last came the great day when news arrived that the Peace of Westphalia had been signed and the war had come to an end. The Elector of Saxony at once ordered Thanksgiving Services to be held in every church, and also selected a text from which ministers were to preach, Ecclesiasticus 50: 22; " Now bless ye the God of all, Who everywhere doeth great things, Who exalteth our days from the womb, and dealeth with us according to His mercy. May He grant us joyful hearts, and may peace be in our days for ever."

A splendid text for the occasion, and one which so struck Martin Rinkart that, as he pondered over it, its words gradually shaped themselves into the form of a hymn, which was doubtless sung at his own Thanksgiving Service, has been translated into other languages, and is now used everywhere. Its notes of gladness are intensified when we remember the horrors of war which its author had experienced, and the close of which it first commemorated. How well Rinkart enshrined the text in the hymn can be seen from the first verse, as translated by Miss Winkworth:

Now thank we all our God
    With hearts and hands, and voices,
Who wondrous things hath done,
    In whom His world rejoices;
Who from our mother's arms
    Hath blessed us on our way
With countless gifts of love,
    And still is ours to-day.

## The Bishop's Mistake

"The origin of English hymns," it has been said, "lies in the paraphrases," or the rendering of passages of Scripture in metrical form for singing. At the Reformation the English Bible seemed to men to have in its words the only security from human error. Hence the long series of Metrical Psalms, which until the end of the seventeenth century alone were used for public praise. Other passages of Scripture were gradually used in this way, some most absurdly, as for instance, the production of a Metrical Version of the Genealogies!

This practice, however, gave rise in later years to some of our most beautiful hymns, one of which is Bishop Wordsworth's " Gracious Spirit, Holy Ghost," which, when read in full, is seen to be a fine paraphrase of 1 Cor. 13, St. Paul's great panegyric of Love. But the two verses which make this so clear are omitted in nearly every hymn-book, thus mutilating the paraphrase entirely; namely:

> Faith that mountains could remove,
> Tongues of earth or heaven above,
> Knowledge—all things—empty prove
> Without heavenly love.

> Though I as a martyr bleed,
> Give my goods the poor to feed,
> All in vain, if love I need;
> Therefore, give me love.

But the seventh stanza is the most remarkable of all, from the fact that the words of the good Bishop therein are absolutely contradictory of the passage he is paraphrasing! St. Paul having described the transitoriness of prophecies and tongues and knowledge, declares that, in contrast to these, the three graces of Faith, Hope, and Love will remain for ever; " But now," he writes, " *abideth* (that is, continueth for ever) faith, hope, love, these three." But the Bishop's hymn states that both faith and hope will disappear in eternity, and that only love will abide!

13

Faith will vanish into sight;
Hope be emptied in delight;
Love in heaven will shine more bright;
    Therefore give us love.

## The Snowy Sunday

It is, perhaps, not very usual to have snow in April, but April 19, 1872, was a snowy Sunday, and Frances Ridley Havergal, then staying at Winterdyne and not very strong, was unable on that account to accompany her friends to church. She remained in bed, only asking for her Prayer Book to be brought to her, as she always liked to follow the services for the day.

On returning from church, Mr. Shaw, with whom she was staying, heard the sound of the piano, and found Miss Havergal playing.

" Why, Frances," he said, " I thought you were upstairs!"

" Yes," replied Miss Havergal, "but I had my Prayer Book, and in the Psalms for to-day I read, '*Tell it out among the heathen that the Lord is King.*' I thought. ' What a splendid first line!' and then words and music came rushing in to me. There it is all written out." With these words she handed Mr. Shaw her manuscript, rapidly written out with the neatness of copperplate—words, music, harmonies, all complete. It will be remembered that Miss Havergal was using her Prayer Book, not her Bible, the translation of Psalm 96 : 10 being different in the latter.

Miss Havergal's words have a splendid ring about them, and her music is as stirring as her words, but,

14

as will be seen from the first verse, the metre is so unusual that the use of the hymn has been distinctly limited on that account:

> Tell it out among the heathen that the Lord is King;
> Tell it out! Tell it out!
> Tell it out among the nations, bid them shout and sing;
> Tell it out! Tell it out!
> Tell it out with adoration that He shall increase;
> That the mighty King of Glory is the King of Peace:
> Tell it out with jubilation, though the waves may roar,
> That He sits above the water-flood a King for evermore.

## The Sunday School Lesson

Miss Mary A. Baker, the authoress of the well-known hymn beginning " Master, the tempest is raging," had been passing through a sad and trying experience. Her beloved and only brother had journeyed to the South in the hope of being restored to health. There, a thousand miles from home, he grew rapidly worse; Miss Baker herself was ill and could not go to him, and after a fortnight's suffering he died. Miss Baker, although a Christian, says that she became " wickedly rebellious " under this bereavement, and actually began to doubt God's love and care. But presently the Master Himself spoke to the restless, troubled heart, and she passed into a new and deeper peace and trust.

Soon after this, Miss Baker was asked to write some hymns on a series of Sunday School lessons then being studied and taught, one of which was on " Christ Stilling the Tempest." The hymn which she wrote on that theme not only embodied the teaching of the lesson,

15

but bore within its bosom the record of her own personal experience, which is clearly set forth in the second verse:

> Master with anguish of spirit,
>   I bow in my grief to-day;
> The depths of my sad heart are troubled;
>   Oh, waken and save, I pray!
> Torrents of sin and of anguish
>   Sweep o'er my sinking soul;
> And I perish! I perish! dear Master;
> Oh, hasten, and take control.

## The Dissatisfied Worshipper

In the year 1694 a young fellow of twenty, whose parents lived at Southampton, returned home from a Nonconformist Academy in London, and joined in worship in a Southampton chapel. The hymn book in use in this chapel was one edited by the Rev. W. Barton, a Nonconformist minister of Leicester, and was one of the first collection of hymns, as distinct from psalms, in the English language. The young worshipper, however, was very dissatisfied with the hymns contained in this book, and went so far as to make a complaint about them, upon which he was challenged to produce anything better. Quite unabashed, he accepted the challenge and set to work to compose a hymn himself, the first of an enormous series of such compositions which were destined to enrich the whole Church of God.

The young man was Isaac Watts, and this first hymn was founded upon the fifth chapter of the Book of the Revelation, beginning, "Behold the glories of the Lamb." This hymn proved so acceptable to the congregation that he was requested to write more, which he did during the two years he remained at home, the hymns being written out and sung in the chapel from manuscript. Among them was the favourite hymn commencing " There is a land of pure delight," which is said to have been suggested by the view across Southampton Water.

## The Dialogue Hymn

Everybody is familiar with the beautiful hymn, based upon Rev. 7: 12–17, which begins " Lo! round the throne at God's right hand," or sometimes " Lo! round the throne a glorious band," which was written by Cotterill, and appears in his Selections of Hymns, published in 1810. But Cotterill's hymn is not original, it is really an adaptation of a hymn written by the famous Rowland Hill nearly thirty years before. The peculiarity about this hymn, as Rowland Hill wrote it, is that it is cast in the form of a dialogue, one verse asking a question and the next giving the reply, probably a unique form for a hymn to take. Here are the first two verses:

> Q.  Exalted high at God's right hand,
> Nearer the throne than cherubs stand,
> With glory crowned in white array,
> My wondering soul says, Who are they?

> A.  These are the saints beloved of God,
> Washed are their robes in Jesus' blood
> More spotless than the purest white,
> They shine in uncreated light.

17

## *The New Year's Bells*

As the hour of midnight struck on New Year's Day, 1859, the bells of St. Nicholas' Church, Worcester, of which the Rev. W. H. Havergal was then rector, burst out into a merry peal. The Rector's daughters, Maria and Frances, were sleeping together in the Rectory close by, and Maria roused her sister to listen to the bells, at the same time quoting to her, as a New Year's motto, the text " As thy days thy strength shall be."

Frances Havergal did not reply for a few minutes, and then gave back to her sister the same beautiful thought in the form of two verses, which she had composed in those few moments of silence. Her sister was so pleased with them, that the next day the authoress added two more verses to those of the night before.

The four verses form a very beautiful hymn, which appears in a number of American hymn books, and is well worthy a place in our English hymnals, though none seem to have included it. The readers of these pages can judge for themselves of its worth :

> " As thy days thy strength shall be!"
> This should be enough for thee,
> He who knows thy frame will spare
> Burdens more than thou canst bear.
>
> When thy days are veiled in night,
> Christ shall give thee heavenly light;
> Seem they wearisome and long,
> Yet in Him thou shalt be strong.

Cold and wintry though they prove,
Thine, the sunshine of His love;
Or, with fervid heat oppressed,
In His shadow thou shalt rest.

When thy days on earth are past,
Christ shall call thee home at last,
His redeeming love to praise,
Who hath strengthened all thy days.

## The Application of the Sermon

Quite a number of our well-known hymns had their origin in the curious device of a famous Nonconformist minister, some two centuries ago, for riveting the lessons of his sermon on the minds of his congregation. These lessons he put together in the form of a hymn, and at the end of his sermon made his congregation sing it.

Hymn-books were unknown in those days, nor could many of his hearers have read them had they possessed them; he therefore gave out his hymn, line by line, each line being sung as he announced it. But one member of his congregation, who could both read and write, used to copy down these hymns as Philip Doddridge recited them from the pulpit, and thus they were preserved for the use of countless thousands of worshippers in after years.

Let us in thought join Doddridge's congregation one Sunday morning in his chapel at Northampton. He reads a lesson from Luke 12: 35–38, and then proceeds to impress upon his hearers the solemn and striking teaching of this wonderful passage. It is *they* who are the servants of the Lord Christ, expectant of

19

His Second Advent, and with lighted lamps and girded loins watching for His Coming, which even then for them was close at hand. Let each one be ready for that hour, for great indeed would be the reward of watch-fulness; not only the rapturous vision of the Lord, and the crown of glory, but even the participation at the King's Own table of the feast prepared by His Own Hand. And then, line by line, the now well-known words are sung for the first time:

> Ye servants of the Lord,
>   Each in his office wait,
> Observant of His heavenly word,
>   And watchful at His gate.

It will be seen, by reference to the hymn, how it drove home the lessons of the passage from which Doddridge preached. Some five hundred hymns were the work of Doddridge's pen, among which are " Awake, my soul, stretch every nerve "; " Hark, the glad sound, the Saviour comes "; " My God, and is Thy Table spread "; " O God of Bethel, by Whose Hand "; and " Oh happy day that fixed my choice."

## Formed from a Single Word

The well-known hymn " O come, O come, Emmanuel," has a curious origin. In the ancient Church it was the custom to sing a short sentence which fitted in with the particular Church season or festival immediately before and after the Magnificat. This was called the Antiphon. The Antiphon sung in this way during the season of Advent consisted of only one word, a long drawn out " O! ", like a cry of distress, meant to indicate the intense longing of the Church for her Lord's Return. This was called " The Great O of Advent."

After a time, someone added to this single word some of the titles ascribed in Scripture to our Lord, together with a brief prayer, such as " O Emmanuel, come and save us "; " O Key of David, unlock the prison house "; " O Dayspring, come and give us light," etc. One of these was chanted on each of the seven days before Christmas, and if any reader will turn to the calendar for December, at the beginning of his Prayer Book, he will find printed in it on December 16 the words " *O Sapientia*," the Latin for " O Wisdom," the two words with which the first of the Advent Antiphon began, and which were sung on that day.

Later still, some person turned five or more of these Antiphons into a Latin hymn, and finally Dr. Neale translated that hymn into English, his translation finding a place in every hymn-book of any repute in the present day.

## My First Hymn

It may be of some interest, perhaps, to the readers of these pages to know the circumstances which led to the publication of my first hymn. I was then on the staff of the Church Missionary Society in London, in connection with which Society was the world-wide organi-

zation, the Gleaners' Union (as it was then called:
now "Missionary Service League"), founded by Dr.
Eugene Stock, and which always held its anniversary on All Saints' Day, November 1. At this
anniversary the Union's Motto Text for the following
year was announced and for the year 1897 the Motto
Text which had been selected was threefold, viz. :

"When the burnt-offering began, the song of the Lord began
    also" (2 Chron. 29: 27).
"A living sacrifice" (Rom. 12: 1).
"A new song" (Psa. 40: 3)

On a Sunday afternoon, about a week before the
anniversary, I was sitting in my drawing-room and
thinking over this striking motto, chosen by Dr. Stock
himself, and known, of course, to us at headquarters,
when the idea suddenly flashed into my mind to jot
down in verse some of the thoughts which it suggested.
I did this, and the next morning, thinking that Dr.
Stock, who then was our Editorial Secretary, might care
to publish the lines in one of the C.M.S. magazines, I
went to his room, which was empty, and laid them on
his table.

Of their use as a hymn I had never dreamed, but
Dr. Stock, coming in and finding them, was at once
struck, not merely by the lines, but by the fact that they
exactly fitted the beautiful tune "Ruth." He had them
printed off at once as a leaflet, and to my intense sur-
prise they were sung at the forthcoming anniversary.
Except for this generous appreciation and action of Dr.
Stock's, it is probable that I should never have tried

22

to do any work as a hymn-writer. The first hymn has been included in several collections, including *Hymns of Consecration and Faith,* and I may, perhaps, venture to quote the first and last verses:

In the cleansed temple,
  On the festal day,
When the whole burnt-offering
  On the altar lay—
Then the priestly trumpets
  Echoed loud and long,
Then ten thousand voices
  Sang the Lord's own song.

Grant us, blessed Master,
  So to yield to Thee
Body, soul, and spirit,
  Our burnt-offering free—
That in Thine own temple,
  With the white-robed throng,
We may join for ever
  In the glad new song.

## After the Sermon

Dr. Thomas Hastings was a musician as well as a hymn writer. Taking the aggregate number of American hymnals published during the last half of the nineteenth century, it has been found that more hymns written by him are included than those of any other American writer. Yet not one of his hymns can be said to be of the highest merit! He has told us the story of the hymn of which the first verse runs,

Return, O wanderer, to thy home,
  Thy Father calls for thee;
No longer now an exile roam,
  In guilt and misery.
    Return! Return!

23

Dr. Hastings says that it was written after hearing a striking revival sermon on the Prodigal Son preached by the Rev. Mr. Kint, at a large meeting where two hundred converts were present. The preacher, at the close of his sermon, appealed to the congregation with great tenderness, exclaiming, "Sinner, come home! come home!" "It was easy," says Dr. Hastings, "afterwards to write, 'Return, O wanderer.'"

## The Three Periods of Life

Caroline Maria Noel, daughter of the Rev. and Hon. Baptist W. Noel, wrote her first hymn at the age of seventeen, which was followed by the writing of several others during the next three years. On reaching her twentieth birthday she ceased to write anything for another period of twenty years, which brought her to the age of forty. Then, for a third period of twenty years, she once more took her pen and wrote. It was during this third period that she composed the most famous of all her hymns, the Processional for Ascension Day, based upon the great passage Phil. 2: 5–11, and beginning,

At the Name of Jesus
  Every knee shall bow,
Every tongue confess Him
  King of Glory now;
'Tis the Father's pleasure
  We should call Him Lord,
Who from the beginning
  Was the mighty Word.

## Written on Glass

One Whit-Sunday, at Hoddesdon, in Hertfordshire, a lady was sitting in her bedroom, and thinking over the sermon she had heard that morning in church. She had in her desk a number of hymns intended for publication, and, as she sat meditating, the lines of a new hymn began to form themselves in her mind. Neither pencil nor paper were handy, but she was sitting near her window, so with a diamond ring which was on her finger she wrote the verses, one by one, on a pane of the glass, beginning,

> Our Blest Redeemer, ere He breathed
> His tender last farewell,
> A Guide, a Comforter bequeathed
> With us to dwell.

Miss Harriet Auber wrote one verse which is omitted from many hymn-books at the present day, viz.:

> He came in tongues of living flame
> To teach, convince, subdue,
> All-powerful as the wind He came,
> As viewless too.

The words of the hymn remained written on the bedroom window for many years, but after the death of the authoress the pane of glass was cut out and stolen.

## The Sick-bed

Sixty years ago a man was ill in bed at Bristol. William Chatterton Dix was an insurance agent, and an earnest, godly Churchman. When the Feast of the Epiphany came round (January 6, 1860) he was, of course, unable to go to church, so as he lay in bed he read to himself the Epiphany Gospel (Matt. 2: 1–12).

Pondering over the passage, it seemed to him to be fraught with real practical teaching for ourselves, and the Wise Men became to him examples to be followed by us. So before he slept that night he had turned these ideas into poetry, and given the world that lovely Epiphany hymn, each verse setting forth, first, the Wise Men's example, and then how we can imitate them:

> As with gladness men of old
> Did the guiding star behold;
> As with joy they hailed its light,
> Leading onward, beaming bright;
> So, most gracious Lord, may we
> Evermore be led to Thee.

## In the Baker's Shop

To James Montgomery the Church of Christ owes a number of the most familiar and best-loved hymns, such as " Hail to the Lord's Anointed," " Songs of praise the angels sang," and " For ever with the Lord." Of the four hundred hymns from his pen, no less than one hundred are still in use. The earliest of all was a metrical version of Psa. 113, beginning " Servants of God, His praise proclaim," though in some hymn-books it appears with the first line of the last verse as the opening of the hymn—" Servants of God! in joyful lays."

26

The curious thing about this first hymn is that at the time he wrote it Montgomery had run away from the Moravian School at Fulneck at the age of seventeen, and had entered the employ of a man named Lockwood, at Mirfield, who was known as " The Fine Bread Baker." In his shop, Montgomery waited behind the counter for about a year and a half, but there was little to do, and the employment was anything but congenial. He seems, therefore, to have spent a good deal of his time in writing poetry, including a long poem called " Alfred ", and it was then that he, one of the most famous hymn writers of our land, produced his first hymn.

## Beside the Death-bed

In August 1875, the Rev. E. H. Bickersteth, then Vicar of Christ Church, Hampstead, was staying with his family in a house at Harrogate, facing the Stray. One Sunday morning he heard Canon Gibbon, the Vicar of Harrogate, preach from the text " Thou wilt keep him in perfect peace, whose mind is stayed on Thee " (Isa. 26: 3), in which he alluded to the beauty of the phrase " perfect peace " as rendering the repeated word " Peace, peace " in the original Hebrew.

That Sunday afternoon Mr. Bickersteth went to visit a dying relative in Harrogate, Archdeacon Hill of Liverpool, and finding him somewhat troubled in mind, he took a sheet of paper, and wrote there and then his beautiful hymn, " Peace, perfect peace," afterwards reading it to the dying man.

Mr. Bickersteth's son states that he still remembers his father coming in to tea that Sunday afternoon, saying " Children, I have written you a hymn ", and reading it to them at the meal. His custom at that particular meal on Sundays was to ask each of his family to repeat a hymn, doing the same himself or reading out some new composition of his own.

Later on, one of Mr. Bickersteth's sisters drew his attention to the fact that his hymn, beautiful as it was, contained no reference to the trial of physical suffering. " That is soon remedied ", he replied, and, taking up an envelope, wrote on the back,

> Peace, perfect peace, 'mid suffering's sharpest throes?
> The sympathy of Jesus breathes repose.

These additional lines, however, were either written too late or did not carry the same appeal as the rest; at any rate, they do not appear in any of the best-known hymn-books as a part of the hymn.

In singing the hymn it is all but impossible to convey the fact that it really consists of question and answer, the question being in the first line of each verse (except the last) while the second line gives the reply thus :

> Q.  Peace, perfect peace, in the dark world of sin?
> A.  The Blood of Jesus whispers peace within.

But no music has ever yet been written to this hymn—perhaps cannot be—which indicates this fact, although the author knows of one composer who added to his tune the odd direction " To be sung in an enquiring spirit "—without, however, any indication of how this was to be done! Probably nearly everyone, therefore, in singing the hymn, will continue to take the first line of each verse merely as a statement of fact.

Chapter 2

## *Following Conversion*

The brothers Wesley owed much, in the spiritual crisis of their lives, to the help given them by Peter Bohler, a Moravian. When he left them Charles Wesley went to reside with a poor brazier named Bray, whom he described as knowing " nothing but Christ ", and who so continued the work Bohler had begun that Charles Wesley's conversion soon took place. This was on May 21, 1738, John Wesley's conversion following almost immediately. Charles Wesley gives the account of his writing, two days after his conversion, one of two hymns in commemoration of that event, of which the first lines run,

> Where shall my wondering soul begin?
> How shall I all to heaven aspire?

The author says: " At nine I began a hymn of my conversion, but was persuaded to break off for fear of pride. Mr. Bray coming in, encouraged me to proceed in spite of Satan. I prayed Christ to stand by me, and finished the hymn. Upon my afterwards

30

showing it to Mr. Bray, the devil threw in a fiery dart, suggesting that it was wrong, and I had displeased God.

" My heart sank within me; when, casting my eyes upon a Prayer Book, I met with an answer for him: ' Why boasteth thou thyself, thou tyrant, that thou canst do mischief?' Upon this I clearly perceived that it was a device of the enemy to keep back glory from God. Least of all would he have us tell what things God has done for our souls, so tenderly does he guard us from pride."

This account of the writing of the hymn is remarkably reflected in its lines. The first two verses express the joy of the forgiven soul, and it was then that probably Wesley was tempted to give up his task, the next verse harmonizing exactly with his determination to continue, as it exclaims,

> And shall I slight my Father's love?
>   Or basely fear His gifts to own?
> Unmindful of His favours prove?
>   Shall I, the hallowed cross to shun,
> Refuse His righteousness to impart,
> By hiding it within my heart?

## On the Way to Work

The well-known hymn beginning,

> My hope is built on nothing less
> Than Jesus' Blood and Righteousness,

was written by Edward Mote, at that time engaged in business in London, and afterwards a Sussex Baptist minister, being for the last twenty-six years of his life pastor at Horsham, in Sussex. Mr. Mote gave the following story of the way the hymn was written: "One morning it came into my mind, as I went to labour, to write a hymn on 'The Gracious Experience of a Christian.' As I went up Holborn I had the chorus,

> "On Christ the solid Rock I stand,
> All other ground is sinking sand.

"In the day I had four first verses complete, and wrote them off. On the Sabbath following I met brother King as I came out of Lisle Street Meeting, who informed me that his wife was very ill, and asked me to call and see her.

"I had an early tea, and called afterwards. He said that it was his usual custom to sing a hymn, read a portion, and engage in prayer, before he went to meeting. He looked for his hymn-book, but could find it nowhere. I said I had some verses in my pocket; if he liked, we would sing them. We did; and his wife enjoyed them so much that, after service, he asked me, as a favour, to leave a copy of them for her. I went home, and by the fireside composed the last two verses, wrote the whole off, and took them to sister King.

"As these verses so met the dying woman's case, my attention to them was the more arrested, and I had a thousand printed for distribution. I sent one to the *Spiritual Magazine*, without my initials, and it appeared in due course."

It will be observed that Mr. Mote describes the writing of *six* verses, in which form the hymn first appeared, the first verse beginning,

> Nor earth, nor hell, my soul can move.

But in its modern form only four verses, as a rule, are used. The original, in the author's *Hymns of Praise*, published in 1836, is entitled " The Immutable Basis of a Sinner's Hope." Bishop Bickersteth called it " a grand hymn of faith."

## The Forgotten Meal

The hymn, which appears in several hymnals, beginning,

> How bright appears the morning star,
> With mercy beaming from afar.

is a translation from the German, the author being Dr. Philipp Nicolai, who also wrote " Sleepers, wake, a voice is calling ", a hymn of the very first rank, and well-known from its use as a Chorale in Mendelssohn's oratorio " St. Paul." But these hymns were written at Unna, in Westphalia, a place of which Nicolai was pastor, during the great pestilence which raged there from July, 1597, to the following January, and in which 1,300 persons perished.

" How bright appears the morning star " was composed by Nicolai one morning when he was in great distress and tribulation in his study. From that distress, and from the death which surrounded him, he rose in spirit to his Redeemer and Saviour, and as he gazed up to Him in ardent love there welled forth from his heart this beautiful hymn, full of the Saviour's love and of the joys of heaven. So entirely absorbed was he in this holy exaltation that he forgot everything else, including his noontide meal, and allowed nothing to disturb him until he had completed the hymn, which was not finished until three hours after midday.

## In the Corner of the Field

When, in the year 1765, the poet Cowper had recovered his balance of mind, his friends made him an annual allowance, sufficient, in addition to his own small income, for his maintenance, and left him to follow his own devices. He resolved to retire both from the business and from the society of the world, and, after vainly trying to get nearer Cambridge, was taken by his brother John to some lodgings which the latter had found for him at Huntingdon.

No sooner had his brother left him than Cowper was overcome with feelings of depression and loneliness. He compares himself to " a traveller in the midst of an inhospitable desert, without friend to comfort, or a guide to direct him." He goes on to say, " I walked forth towards the close of the day, and in this melancholy frame of mind, and having wandered about a mile from the town, I found my heart at length so powerfully drawn towards the Lord that, having found a retired and lonely nook in the corner of a field, I kneeled down under a bank and poured forth my complaints before Him.

"It pleased my Saviour to hear me, so that this oppression was taken off, and I was enabled to trust in Him that careth for the stranger. But," he adds, "this was not all. He did for me more than either I had asked or thought."

The following day was Sunday, June 23, and Cowper attended Divine Service for the first time since his recovery. He was immensely impressed by two things; the reading of the parable of the Prodigal Son, and by the intense devotion of one of the worshippers. How little that worshipper ever could have dreamed of the help that came through his own earnestness and reverence to another soul!

Immediately after church Cowper retired once more to his quiet nook in the field, and there experienced a far greater blessing even than that of the previous day. "How shall I express", he says, "what the Lord did for me, except by saying that He made all His goodness to pass before me! I seemed to speak to Him face to face, as a man conversing with his friend."

There can be little doubt that this sacred corner of the field was the birthplace of Cowper's touching hymn, the second verse of which bears clear reference to that hour of blest communion with his Lord:

> Far from the world, O Lord, I flee,
>     From strife and tumult far;
> From scenes where Satan wages still
>     His most successful war.

> The calm retreat, the silent shade,
>   With prayer and praise agree;
> And seem, by Thy sweet bounty, made
>   For those who follow Thee.

## The Night of his Conversion

Dr. G. F. Pentecost was once conducting a service in his church at Brooklyn, followed by an after-meeting. In the congregation was a cultured gentleman, Nathaniel Norton, who had never acknowledged himself to be a Christian until that evening, when at the close of the after-meeting he stood up and publicly confessed his acceptance of Christ. That same night, on his return home, he sat down and wrote a hymn, which was afterwards given to Mr. G. C. Stebbins, then assisting Dr. Pentecost, by whom it was set to music, being afterwards widely used. It began thus:

> " Come unto Me!" It is the Saviour's Voice—
> The Lord of Life. Who bids thy heart rejoice;
> O weary heart, with heavy cares opprest,
> " Come unto Me," and I will give you rest.

## Heard in a Dream

A remarkable experience in hymn-writing was that of Prebendary Edward Harland. His hymn " O Heavenly Jerusalem, Thou city of the Lord," is not widely known, but its origin is truly extraordinary. During the night of October 5, 1862, the author was asleep, and dreamed that he saw the heavenly choirs, numbering ten thousand times ten thousand, entering a glorious temple, and singing a hymn of which he could distinguish the very words. He awoke from his dream and, rising from bed, struck a light, and on the back of a letter wrote down the words he had heard in his dream, then once more retired to rest.

The next morning he found on his dressing-table, and afterwards published, the hymn which had been given to him in this remarkable way, the first verse of which runs thus:

> O heavenly Jerusalem,
>   Thou city of the Lord,
> What holy joy and transport
>   Does thy sweet name afford!
> Jerusalem, Jerusalem,
>   Enthroned in light above!
> Where Jesus reigns in glory,
>   The Saviour Whom I love.

## On the Gravel Walk

In 1878 a young Yale student was present at one of Mr. Moody's meetings in America, and was spoken to at the after-meeting by a gentleman, who afterwards accompanied him to the gate of his home, urging him to accept Christ and to decide the question that very night. The young student was greatly impressed.

As the young man neared the house he stopped and drew a deep line with his cane on the gravel walk. "Now," he said, "I must decide this question to-night. If I cross this line, my life shall be for Christ; if I go round it, it will be for the world." For some half-hour he stood on the walk with the line at his feet, until at last he cried, " O God, help me to decide aright," and strode over the line, going at once to his father's room to tell him of his decision to be a Christian.

The father, who was a minister, told the story from the platform at Mr. Moody's meeting the following day, many of the audience being moved to tears, while Mr. E. H. Phelps, a newspaper proprietor, published it the next morning. In another town of the same State, Mrs. Ellen K. Bradford read of the incident in the paper and, sitting down, immediately wrote the hymn beginning,

> Oh, tender and sweet was the Master's Voice,
>     As He lovingly called to me;
> " Come over the line! It is only a step—
>     I am waiting, My child, for thee ";

followed by the well-known chorus,

> " Over the line!" hear the sweet refrain!
>     Angels are chanting the heavenly strain;
> " Over the line "—why should I remain
>     With a step between me and Jesus?

Posted to the editor, Mr. Phelps, he at once set it to music, and gave it to Mr. Sankey, who both used and published it. It has been the means of the conversion of thousands of souls all over the world.

## In the Back Room

It was New Year's Eve in the year 1866. The shades

of evening were falling where, in a little back room of Shareshill Parsonage, without carpet, without fire, there sat writing, despite the cold, one of our greatest hymn-writers, Frances Ridley Havergal. She had been feeling that she had not written anything specially in praise of Christ, but a great longing to do so possessed her, and she was now writing one of her least-known hymns—as perhaps she would have wished it to be, for, she tells us, she was writing just for her Lord alone. The first verse of the hymn, which she entitled " Adoration," is as follows:

O Master, at Thy feet
I bow in rapture sweet!
Before me, as in darkening glass,
Some glorious outlines pass,
Of love, and truth, and holiness, and power;
I own them Thine, O Christ, and bless Thee for this hour.

Miss Havergal said that " Master " was her favourite title for our Lord, because it implied rule and submission, which is what love craves. " Men ". she writes, " may feel differently, but a true woman's submission is inseparable from deep love."

## The Seven Sermons

During the winter of 1867 Henry Moorhouse, a young Englishman, known as the " Boy Preacher," offered to preach for Mr. Moody in his church at Chicago. Mr. Moody, although by no means anxious that he should do so, thinking him too young for preaching, finally consented. The result was that the place became packed with people for seven nights in succession, so great was the attractiveness of Moorhouse's preaching, and on each night the preacher took the same text—John 3; 16—and preached on the same subject—the Love of God for the sinner. This course of addresses, Moody says, altered in many respects his own style of preaching, and they also impressed very deeply Mr. P. P. Bliss, who wrote, as an outcome of the lessons he had learned from Moorhouse, the hymn beginning,

> Whosoever heareth, shout, shout the sound!
> Send the blessed tidings all the world around,

which he himself used to sing with special emphasis laid upon the word " Whosoever ".

## One Year after Conversion

One of our best-known hymns is that beginning,

> Oh, for a thousand tongues to sing
> My great Redeemer's praise.

But the original hymn began otherwise. It was written by Charles Wesley on the first anniversary of his conversion to God, which took place on Sunday, May 21, 1738, and began,

> Glory to God, and praise, and love.

the heading being " For the Anniversary Day of One's Conversion ". The author's brother, John Wesley, however, very much shortened the original hymn, which consisted of no fewer than eighteen verses, and began the new version with the author's seventh verse, as every one sings it now.

In this form it stands prominent as the first hymn in *The Methodist Hymn Book*. It appears that this seventh verse sprang from a conversion which Charles Wesley had with Peter Bohler, the Moravian, on the subject of praising Christ, during which Bohler remarked, " Had I a thousand tongues I would praise Him with them all ", thus giving Wesley the idea of the present opening lines of the hymn.

One of the expressions in this hymn provoked at one time some little controversy, namely, the line that runs,

> He breaks the power of cancelled sin.

for which some have substituted " death and sin," or " reigning sin," but the line is now generally accepted as Wesley wrote it.

## While the Vision Lasted

The Rev. W. O. Cushing had a curious experience in the year 1875, to which is due the composition of a very favourite hymn. While holding communion with God, there suddenly dawned upon him a vision of the heavenly country. He seemed to be looking down upon a great river whose waters rolled beneath him, while on the further bank he gazed upon a glorious land, its hills and valleys spread before him in peaceful beauty. It seemed to him, he says, more

beautiful than words could describe, while, as he gazed
entranced, there came to his lips the words,

> Beautiful valley of Eden,
>   Sweet is thy noontide calm;
> Over the hearts of the weary
>   Breathing thy waves of balm.

As he wrote down the lines of the hymn, the vision
still seemed to float before his eyes, and not until
the lines were completed did it slowly fade away.

## The Midnight Hour of Reconsecration

One of the most beautiful and best-loved hymns
in existence is that by Miss Frances Ridley Havergal,
beginning,

> Take my life, and let it be
> Consecrated, Lord, to Thee,

which has been translated, not only into a number
of European languages, but even into several of Asia
and Africa. The striking account of the writing of
this hymn is thus given by Miss Havergal herself:

" Perhaps you will be interested to know the origin
of the consecration hymn " Take my life ". I went
for a little visit of five days (to Areley House). There
were ten persons in the house, some unconverted and
long prayed for, some converted but not rejoicing
Christians. He gave me the prayer ' Lord give me
ALL in this house.' And He just did. Before I left
the house every one had got a blessing. The last night
of my visit, after I had retired, the governess asked

me to go to the two daughters. They were crying. Then and there both of them trusted and rejoiced. It was nearly midnight. I was too happy to sleep, and passed most of the night in praise and renewal of my own consecration; and these little couplets formed themselves and chimed in my heart one after another, till they finished with ' *Ever,* ONLY, *All for Thee*!' "

Miss Havergal always sang this hymn to her father's tune, " Patmos ", and the desire both of herself and her family was that in any publication including the hymn this same tune should be associated with it. This wish has, however, been almost universally disregarded by compilers, the tune most frequently appearing with the hymn being that known as " Mozart ".

Chapter 3

## Lost at Sea

In 1874 a large French steamer, the *Ville de Havre*, was on her homeward voyage from America, when in mid-ocean a collision with a sailing vessel took place, the steamer sinking in half an hour, with the loss of almost all on board. A Mrs. Spafford, the wife of a lawyer in Chicago, was a passenger, accompanied by her four children. On being told that the vessel was rapidly foundering, she knelt with her children in prayer, asking God that if possible they might be saved, or be made willing to die, if such was His Will.

A few minutes later the ship went down, and the children were lost. Mrs. Spafford, however, was rescued by a sailor, who, rowing over the spot where the vessel had disappeared, found her floating in the water, and ten days later she was landed at Cardiff. " Saved alone ", a message which Mr. Spafford, himself an earnest Christian, had framed and hung in his office.

44

Two years later Messrs. Moody and Sankey were staying with Mr. and Mrs. Spafford for some weeks, and during that visit Mr. Spafford wrote, in commemoration of the death of his children, that hymn, with its triumphant chorus, which has become such a favourite the world over, and in the first lines of which the reference to the great grief of his life is clearly discernible:

> When peace, like a river, attendeth my way,
>   When sorrows, like sea billows, roll,
> Whatever my lot, Thou hast taught me to know
>   It is well, it is well with my soul.

It was the greatest comfort to the bereaved parents to know that all four children had been converted to God at one of Mr. Moody's meetings, shortly before the fatal voyage.


## *The Preacher's Last Wish*

A well-known hymn of Montgomery's was inspired by the circumstances attending the death of a Methodist preacher, the Rev. Thomas Taylor, who, preaching on Sunday evening, October 14, 1861, expressed the hope that he would die as an old soldier of Jesus Christ, with his sword in his hand. The following morning he was found dead in bed. With reference to this, Montgomery wrote the hymn headed " The Christian Soldier ", and beginning thus:

" Servant of God, well done!
  Rest from thy loved employ;
The battle fought, the victory won,
  Enter thy Master's joy."
The voice at midnight came;
  He started up to hear;
A mortal arrow pierced his frame;
  He fell, but felt no fear.

Although this hymn appears in some hymn-books in this, or some amended form, yet the reference to the special circumstances of Mr. Taylor's death is too marked for the hymn to be suitable for ordinary use.

## The Missing Member

The president of a certain Young People's Society once chanced to meet a girl of fourteen, poorly dressed and a drunkard's daughter, whom he invited to join the Society and to attend Sunday School. She did this, and attended for a time, but one evening at a consecration meeting, when the Society's roll of members was called, each member responding with a text, there was no response from this girl. Remarking on her absence the president, Mr. J. M. Black, spoke of the sadness of anyone being absent when the names were called of those written in the Lamb's Book of Life, and then added the prayer, " O God, when my own name is called up yonder, may I be there to respond!"

Wanting something suitable to sing on this occasion, Mr. Black searched the hymn-book, but could find nothing, and, after the meeting was ended, on his way home he still kept wishing for such a hymn, when the thought came to him: "Why not write one yourself?" The idea was at once dismissed as impracticable. On reaching home Mrs. Black was questioning her husband as to the cause of his evident trouble, without receiving a reply, when the words of the first stanza of a new hymn came to his mind in full:

When the trumpet of the Lord shall sound, and time shall be no
    more,
  When the morning breaks, eternal, bright and fair;
When the saved of earth shall gather over on the other shore,
  And the roll is called up yonder, I'll be there!

Within fifteen minutes the two following verses were also written down, and then Mr. Black turned to the piano. "I played the music," he says, "just as it is found to-day in the hymn-books, note for note, and I have never dared to change a single word or a note of the song."

## The General's Signal

In October, 1864, during the American Civil War, General Hood, by a skilful manoeuvre, gained the rear of General Sherman's army, and commenced the destruction of the railway to the north. Sherman put his forces in hot pursuit, being especially anxious to save the supplies and principal posts, the largest of which was at Altoona Pass, where General Corse was stationed with fifteen hundred men, and where no less than one and a half million rations were stored.

Hood sent six thousand men under General French to capture the position. The post was completely surrounded and summoned to surrender; on Corse refusing, sharp fight began. the defenders being slowly driven into a small fort on the crest of the hill.

Just as the situation seemed to have become hopeless an officer caught sight of a white flag on the top of a mountain some twenty miles away, and quickly the message was signalled from the one crest to the other, " Hold the fort; I am coming. Sherman." Inspired by this signal of hope and encouragement, the defenders held the place for another three hours, until Sherman's troops appeared and French was obliged to retreat.

Six years later, at a Sunday School meeting at Rockford, in the State of Illinois, Major Whittle related this incident, and immediately the lines of Mr. P. P. Bliss's well-known hymn flashed into the author's mind as he sat among the hearers. The next day, at a meeting conducted by Messrs. Whittle and Bliss in the Y.M.C.A. rooms at Chicago, Mr. Bliss mounted the platform and wrote the chorus of his new hymn on a blackboard:

" Hold the fort, for I am coming,"
Jesus signals still;
Wave the answer back to heaven,
" By Thy grace we will!"

Mr. Bliss then sang the verses of the hymn for the first time, and the audience joined in the chorus.

The popularity of this hymn and stirring refrain was unbounded. The late Lord Shaftesbury said, at Moody and Sankey's farewell meeting in London in 1874, that if Mr. Sankey had done no more than teach the people to sing "Hold the fort", he had conferred an inestimable blessing on the British Empire. Mr. Bliss himself, however, had not a high opinion of his composition, and said, shortly before his death, that he hoped posterity wouid not remember him only as the writer of "Hold the fort", since he believed he had done much better work. Nevertheless, on the monument erected to his memory at Rome, Pennsylvania, appears the inscription:

P. P. BLISS.
AUTHOR OF "HOLD THE FORT."

## The Dying Rector's Message

Some sixty years ago the young Rector of the Church of the Epiphany, Philadelphia, had incurred the resentment of his congregation on account of his bold declarations from the pulpit that to hold a fellow-creature in slavery was a sin. Most of his congregation owned slaves, a common practice in those days, and their indignation was such that the young Rector was obliged to resign his charge.

A large hall in the city was then taken for him by some of his friends, in which he continued his ministry with marked success. One Sunday he preached to a huge gathering of five thousand men from the words (Exod. 10: 11): "Go now, ye that are men, and serve the Lord," and it is said that after the service a thousand of his hearers signed a pledge to yield their lives to God.

On the following Wednesday he was in a barn, where a mule was working a piece of farm machinery; Mr. Tyng went to pat the animal, when a cogwheel caught his sleeve, his arm being dragged into the machine and torn off. On the following Sunday, immediately before his death, he was asked if he desired to send any message to his congregation. He then uttered the memorable words, the last that fell from his lips, " Tell them to stand up for Jesus."

One of his friends, Dr. Duffield, was inspired by this last message from the dying man to write the well-known hymn, " Stand up, stand up for Jesus!" which he read to the congregation after preaching his friend's funeral sermon the next Sunday. One verse of the original hymn, now invariably omitted, had special reference to Mr. Tyng's tragic death :

> Stand up, stand up for Jesus!—
>   Each soldier to his post;
> Close up the broken column
>   And shout throughout the host;
> Make up the loss so heavy
>   In those that still remain;
> And prove to all around you
>   That death itself is gain.

## The Dying Child's Message

Miss Elizabeth Glyde's hymn, " Be with me in the valley", was written under the following circumstances. In the year 1844 the authoress, whose home was at Exeter, her father being a merchant in that city, went to Malvern for the benefit of her health, which was in a critical condition. The doctors there, however, held out no hope of her recovery, and she soon returned home with their sentence of death resting upon her.

On the Sunday after her return Miss Glyde's sister told her of a dying child of fourteen years of age who had sent this message to her teacher: "Tell her that when I came to the valley of the shadow of death Jesus was there to meet me." Inspired by these words of the dying child, the dying woman wrote this hymn, sometimes printed as "Oh, meet me in the valley."

She died on February 15 in the following year, and the hymn was recited by the Rev. John Bristow, when preaching her funeral sermon in Castle Street Chapel, Exeter.

Be with me in the valley,
   When heart and flesh shall fail
And softly, safely lead me on,
   Until within the veil:
Then faith shall turn to gladness
   To find myself with Thee,
And trembling hope shall realise
   Her full felicity.

## The Lights that Failed

At one of Mr. Moody's meetings in America he related the story of a shipwreck on a dark and tempestuous night, when not even a star was visible. A ship was approaching the harbour of Cleveland, with a pilot on board. The captain, noticing only one light as they drew near—that from the light-house—asked the pilot if he was quite sure that it was Cleveland harbour, as other lights should have been burning at the harbour mouth. The pilot replied that he was quite sure, whereupon the captain enquired:

"Where are the lower lights?"

"Gone out, sir," replied the pilot.

"Can you make the harbour, then?" asked the captain; to which the pilot answered:

"We must, sir, or perish."

Bravely the old man steered the vessel upon her course towards safety. But alas! in the darkness of the harbour mouth he missed the channel, the ship struck upon the rocks, and in the stormy waters many lives were lost.

Then Moody made his appeal to his audience: "Brothers, the Master will take care of the great lighthouse! Let us keep the lower lights burning!"

Among Mr. Moody's hearers that night was Mr. P. P. Bliss, the well-known hymn writer, and the striking story at once suggested to him one of his most popular hymns:

Brightly beams our Father's mercy
　From His lighthouse evermore;
But to us He gives the keeping
　Of the lights along the shore.

Let the lower lights be burning!
　Send a gleam across the wave,
　Some poor, fainting, struggling seaman
　You may rescue, you may save.

52

## The Homesick Wife

Nearly a century ago a young Scotsman and his bride left their native land to seek their fortunes in America. In this they were successful, but while they became richer the wife's health began to give way, and it was soon evident that the cause of the trouble was homesickness. "John," she would say to her husband, "I'm wearying for my ain countree," and begged that she might be taken to the coast, so that she could see the ships sailing to her homeland. Her husband acceded to her request, and, disposing of their home in the West, moved to a little cottage on the East Coast. There the homesick wife would sit and watch the ships as they sailed eastward across the ocean to her native land.

But it soon became plain that she was pining away, and her husband, fearing that her death would ensue, sold the new home also, and took her back across the sea to Scotland once more, where she immediately began to improve in health as by a charm, and eventually completely recovered.

This touching story became known to a young American lady, who, although born in America, was of Scottish ancestry, and who had learned something of the Scottish dialect from her old nurse and from her grandfather. Mary Lee was not only a talented woman, but an earnest Christian, and when at the age of twenty-three, she heard the story of the homesick wife, she founded upon it the expression of spiritual longing for the heavenly home, enshrined in the lines which are almost more poem than hymn:

I am far frae my hame, and I'm weary aftenwhiles,
For the langed-for hame-brinin' an' my Father's welcome smiles,
An' I'll ne'er be fu' content until my een do see
The gowden gates o' heaven an' my ain countree.

The earth is flecked wi' floors, mony-tinted, fresh and gay;
The birdies warble blithely, for my Father made them sae;
But these sichts an' these souns will as noething be to me,
When I hear the angels singin' in my ain countree.

## *The Story of the Last Hours*

Montgomery's short, but beautiful hymn. "Father! Thy will, not Mine, be done," was occasioned by the death, at the early age of twenty-eight, of Mr. William B. Rawson, of Wincobank Hall, Sheffield. His widow gave this account of the writing of the hymn: "My beloved husband went to Paradise on July 19, 1829. When Montgomery was here some time afterwards, he asked my dear mother about his last hours, and seemed much affected by hearing of his wonderful peace and resignation, for he had everything to make life desirable. My mother put into our friend's hand a short statement of the closing scene, which he took up with him when he retired for the night, and the next day we found these lines written in pencil on a fly-leaf of the manuscript."

As the hymn, which bears the title " Resignation ", is not very well known, it may be quoted here:

" Father! Thy will, not mine, be done ";
So prayed on earth Thy suffering Son;
So, in His Name, I pray;
The spirit faints, the flesh is weak,
Thy help in agony I seek,
    O take this cup away!

If such be not Thy sovereign Will,
Thy wiser purpose then fulfil;
  My wishes I resign;
Into Thy Hands my soul commend,
On Thee for life or death depend;
  Thy Will be done, not mine.

## The Legacy

The origin of Mr. P. P. Bliss's hymn beginning,

Have you on the Lord believed?
Still there's more to follow,

was rather curious. The author had heard Mr. Moody relating the story of a very poor man, who was the inheritor of a great fortune, but the legacy was committed to the trust of the minister of the inheritor's parish, to be given to the man at the minister's discretion.

Knowing the peril which always attends the sudden acquisition of wealth, and fearing that if the man came into the immediate possession of the whole fortune it might easily be squandered, the minister sent him only a comparatively small amount at a time, accompanying each payment with a note to this effect: " This is thine; use it wisely; there is more to follow."

## The Girl's Cry

During some revival meetings in a Scottish town a young girl became anxious about her soul, and going to her own minister enquired how she could be sure of salvation. The minister failed, however, to appre-

55

ciate the poor girl's deep spiritual anxiety, and, after talking to her, bade her go home and read the fifty-third chapter of Isaiah.

But the girl's distress of soul was too great to be allayed by such indefinite advice. Uneducated as she was, she cried out, " Oh, sir, I cannot read: I cannot pray!" and then, throwing up her hands, exclaimed, " Lord Jesus , take me as I am!"

As Mr. Moody used to say in his expressive way, when relating this story, " She had got *it* !"

A lady, who heard of this girl's experience, and of her cry to Christ, embodied them in a hymn which has become very widely known and loved:

> Jesus, my Lord, to Thee I cry;
> Unless Thou help me, I must die;
> Oh, bring Thy free salvation nigh,
> And take me as I am!

How little could the despairing girl have thought that her cry to Christ that day would be re-echoed all round the world, and bring its blessing to numberless other souls!

## The Young Man's Testimony

Professor D. B. Towner, who was musical director of the Moody Bible Institute, was singing at a series of meetings conducted by Mr. Moody at Brockton, in Massachusetts. On one of the nights a young man rose in the meeting to give his testimony, which ran thus : " I am going to trust, and I am going to obey."

Professor Towner wrote down the sentence, and sent it, with its story, to the Rev. J. H. Sammis, a Presbyterian minister, who wrote the well-known chorus enshrining the young man's testimony:

> Trust and obey
> For there's no other way
> To be happy in Jesus
> But to trust and obey.

The hymn itself, beginning, "When we walk with the Lord," and also the tune, were written afterwards.

## In the Jewish Synagogue

Thomas Olivers, one of Whitefield's converts, had led a very profligate life as a shoemaker until his conversion took place, being afterwards accepted by Mr. Wesley as a preacher of the Gospel at the age of twenty-eight. Nearly twenty years later Olivers was on a visit to another Methodist lay preacher, John Bakewell, of Westminster, and while a guest at his house visited the Jewish Synagogue, where he heard a beautiful melody sung by a Rabbi, Signor Leoni.

Olivers was so struck by the music that he immediately decided to write a Christian hymn which would fit the same melody, and enable it to be sung by Methodists; so under Mr. Bakewell's hospitable roof the magnificent hymn was composed which begins with lines possibly suggested by the place in which he had listened to the tune:

The God of Abraham praise,
    Who reigns enthroned above;
Ancient of everlasting days,
    And God of love.

The hymn became so immensely popular that in its second year no less than eight editions were needed, while the tune to which it is set is known by the name of the singer from whose lips it first reached the ears of Olivers.

## Out of a Christmas Story

The Christmas number of *Household Words* for 1836, a magazine of which Charles Dickens was the editor, consisted of a story entitled " The Wreck of the Golden Mary," by Miss Harriet Parr. The story describes the striking of the Golden Mary on an iceberg, and how the passengers, taking to the boats, suffered privations for several days. To while away the time they took it in turns to repeat stories. One of them, a wild youth, named Dick Tarrant, related some of his experiences, in the course of which he said :

" What can it be that brings all these old things over my mind? There's a child's hymn Tom and I used to say at my mother's knee, when we were little ones, keeps running through my thoughts. It's the stars, maybe; there was a little window by my bed that I used to watch them at, a window in my room at home in Cheshire; and if I were ever afraid, as boys will be after reading a good ghost-story, I would keep on saying it till I fell asleep."

" That was a good mother of yours, Dick," replied one of the passengers. " Could you say that hymn now, do you think? Some of us might like to hear it."

" It is as clear in my mind at this minute as if my mother were here listening to me," said Dick. And he repeated :

> Hear my prayer, O Heavenly Father,
> Ere we lay us down to sleep;
> Bid Thine angels, pure and holy,
> Round our bed their vigils keep.

And so through all the verses of this beautiful hymn, which, taken out of this story, first appeared in the *New Congregational Hymn Book* in 1859 and has found a place in many collections since. Not only is its origin so curious, but it is the only hymn ever written by Miss Parr.

## Chapter 4

### *From Hours to Moments*

During the World's Fair at Chicago religious meetings were frequently held, and at one of these the hymn " I need Thee every hour "was sung, when the well-known evangelists, Mr. Henry Varley and Major D. W. Whittle, were present. Mr. Varley remarked to Major Whittle that he did not care very much for the hymn, because he felt he needed Christ every moment of the day and not only every hour. It is open to question whether the criticism was warranted, as the expression " every hour " was probably intended to be equivalent to " always "; however, the remark fastened itself in Major Whittle's mind, and led to his writing the hymn beginning: " Dying with Jesus, by death reckoned mine," and with the chorus obviously founded upon Mr. Varley's words :

> Moment by moment I'm kept in His love;
> Moment by moment I've life from above;
> Looking to Jesus till glory doth shine;
> Moment by moment, O Lord, I am Thine.

## At the Convention

Mr. L. H. Biglow was returning on one occasion from a prayer meeting in company with his blind friend, Miss Fanny Crosby, the well-known hymn writer. The subject brought forward at the prayer meeting by its conductor was " Grace ", and on the way home Mr. Biglow asked his friend to write a hymn thereon. Retiring to an adjoining room, she returned in the course of an hour with the new hymn, which Mr. Biglow placed in a safe with other compositions of Miss Crosby's, where it was apparently forgotten.

Later on Miss Crosby was the guest of Mr. Sankey during the Northfield Summer Conference of 1894, and was asked by him one evening if she would give a short address at the Convention. At first she declined, but afterwards consented to speak for a few minutes. Being led forward to the speaker's desk, Miss Crosby gave a short but earnest address, and then, having finished her remarks, she recited the hymn written at Mr. Biglow's request, beginning:

> Some day the silver cord will break,
> And I no more, as now, shall sing.

In this remarkable fashion the hymn was first made public.

## To Comfort his Mother

There landed in Canada in the year 1845 a young

Irishman named Joseph Scriven, who lived in his adopted country until 1886, when he died at the age of sixty-six. His consecration of his life to Christ was the result of a terrible grief which befell him in his earliest years, the young lady to whom he was engaged being accidentally drowned on the eve of their wedding day. No one had ever known that Scriven was possessed of any poetical gift, until, shortly before his death, a neighbour who was watching beside him during his last illness, found in his room some lines in manuscript which he read with intense delight.

Asking Mr. Scriven how he came to write it, the latter replied that in a time of very special sorrow he had written it to bring comfort to his mother, not intending that any eye but hers should see it. His account of the authorship of the hymn was "The Lord and I did it between us." The first lines of the hymn that met the eye of the delighted neighbour were:

> What a Friend we have in Jesus,
>   All our sins and griefs to bear!
> What a privilege to carry
>   Everything to God in prayer!

## A Christmas Present

Few of those who join on Christmas Day in singing "Christians, awake, salute the happy morn," have any idea that the Christian Church owes this magnificent hymn to the pretty fancy of a young girl. Dolly

Byrom and her father lived in Manchester, more than a century and a half ago, John Byrom being a teacher of shorthand, and also a Jacobite leader.

One day, shortly before Christmas, Byrom asked his daughter what she would like for a Christmas present, and Dolly, knowing that her father sometimes wrote poetry, replied, " Please write me a poem." When she came down on Christmas morning she found on her plate a piece of paper—still preserved in the Library of Cheetham's Hospital, Manchester—on which was written a hymn, headed " Christmas Day, For Dolly."

Soon after, John Wainwright, the organist of Manchester Parish Church, now its cathedral, saw this hymn, and composed for it the tune " Yorkshire ", which we all know so well. On the following Christmas morning Byrom and his daughter were awakened by the sound of singing below their windows; it was Wainwright with his choir, singing Dolly's hymn :

Christians awake, salute the happy morn
Whereon the Saviour of mankind was born.

## The Little Mission Church

In how many magnificent churches, with crowded congregations assembled for the consecration of the building, have the beautiful words been sung :

We love the place, O God,
    Wherein Thine honour dwells,
The joy of Thine abode
    All earthly joy excels.

How different the scene when they were sung for the first time!

Just about a century ago a young naval officer, William Bullock, was ordered to survey the coast of Newfoundland.

An earnest man, the conditions of the settlers there, bereft of any kind of religious worship or instruction, so horrified him that he resigned his post, sought ordination, and went out to Newfoundland again as a missionary of the Society for the Propagation of the Gospel. At a small place named Trinity Bay he built his first little Mission Church, for the consecration of which he wrote this great hymn, and amid such poor surroundings, in that tiny building, were first sung the words which were destined to form one of the great hymns of Christendom.

Bullock, who afterwards became Dean of Halifax, Nova Scotia, wrote two verses which have disappeared from our editions of the hymn, one of which was strikingly appropriate when one remembers his errand there as a pioneer missionary. The words are these:

> We love Thy saints, who come
> Thy mercy to proclaim,
> To call the wanderers home,
> And magnify Thy Name.

Sir H. W. Baker, whose changes in the hymn are now universally adopted, omitted the above verse, which refers to the preacher, and substituted one which pointed instead to the Word read and preached, viz:

We love the Word of life,
The Word that tells of peace
Of comfort in the strife,
And joys that never cease.

## The Publishers' Refusal

Mr. Ira D. Sankey relates that, during the meetings held by Mr. Moody and himself in Great Britain in the years 1873-74, he had frequently sung as a solo the striking poem of Tennyson's, founded on the parable of the Ten Virgins, and commencing,

Late, late, so late, and dark the night and chill,
Late, late, so late, but we can enter still.
Too late! Too late! Ye cannot enter now!

Mr. Sankey was then compiling an edition of his *Sacred Songs and Solos*, and he asked permission to include this poem, but the owners of the copyright refused. Upon this Mr. Sankey asked Dr. H. Bonar if he would write for him a hymn on the same lines, with the result that Dr. Bonar produced the solemn verses in exactly the same metre, and therefore capable of being sung to the same music, beginning,

Yet there is room! The Lamb's bright hall of song,
With its fair glory, beckons thee along!
Room, room! Still room! Oh, enter, enter now!

Thus the world owes one of its most beautiful mission hymns to the publishers' refusal!

## At the Dean's Request

On Whit-Sunday, 1819, a sermon was preached in Wrexham Parish Church, in aid of the Society for

## FROM GREENLAND'S
### FACSIMILE OF HEBER'S

Tune when the Seas were roaring

From Greenland's Icy Mountains,
From India's Coral Strand.
Where africs, sunny fountains
Roll down their Golden Sand,
From many an ancient River
From many a palmy plain.
They call us to deliver
Their land from error's chain

What though the spicy breezes
Blow soft o'er ___ Isle
Though every prospect pleases
And only man is vile.
In vain with lavish kindness.
The gifts of God are strewn.
The Heathen in his blindness
Bows down to wood & stone! —

66

Can we. whose souls are lighted
  With wisdom from on high
Can we to men benighted
  The Lamp of Life deny? —
salvation! yea, Salvation!
  The joyful sound proclaim,
Till each remotest nation
  Has learnd Messiah's name! —

~~Shall~~. waft ye winds the Story.
  and you. Ye waters. roll,
Till. like a sea of glory,
  It spreads from Pole to Pole !.
Till . o'er our ransomd nature,
  The Lamb for sinners slain,
Redeemer. King. Creator.
  In bliss return ~~reign~~ !

67

the Propagation of the Gospel in Foreign Parts, by Dr. Shipley, who was Vicar of Wrexham and also Dean of St. Asaph's. On the same evening was given the first of a series of Sunday Evening Lectures, delivered by the Dean's son-in-law, the Rev. Reginald Heber, then Rector of Hodnet, and afterwards Bishop of Calcutta.

On the previous Saturday evening, when Heber was at the Vicarage, the Dean asked him to write " something for them to sing in the morning ". Upon which Heber left the table where the Dean and other friends were sitting, and going to another part of the room sat down and began to write. After a while the Dean asked him, "What have you written?" whereupon Heber read aloud the first three verses of the greatest of all missionary hymns, which he had then composed, beginning,

> From Greenland's icy mountains,
> From India's coral strands.

" There, there, that will do very well," said the Dean, who evidently had a strong objection to long hymns. "No, no," replied Heber, "the sense is incomplete ", and, sitting down again, wrote the magnificent fourth verse, commencing,

> Waft, waft, ye winds, His story,
> And you, ye waters, roll.

Even then he was not satisfied; "Let me add

another! oh, let me add another!" he repeatedly exclaimed, but in vain; the Dean was inexorable in refusing to allow any further extension of the hymn, which as thus written was sung for the first time in Wrexham Parish Church the next morning.

Heber's original manuscript was filed in the office of the Wrexham printer, and a facsimile of this most interesting document is given on page 66, by the kind permission of Messrs. Hughes and Son, Wrexham, from whom copies can be obtained price threepence, post free. It will be observed, on studying the manuscript, that Heber originally wrote, in the second verse:

The *savage* in his blindness,

which he himself changed to " heathen," making the line much smoother thereby. Also in the third verse the original words of the fifth line are:

Salvation! *yea,* salvation!

instead of the " oh, salvation!" to which we are all accustomed. Later on Heber also altered " Ceylon's isle " to " Java's isle," obviously to correct the accent which falls on the first syllable of the word, and which was therefore faulty in " Ceylon's."

The blurring marks in the second and fourth verses are caused by the printer's file, which pierced the paper at these points.

## *The Sunday School Procession*

Nearly sixty years ago a new curate arrived at Horbury, a village in Yorkshire, just outside Wakefield. As in so many North country places, the march of the Sunday scholars in procession round the parish on Whit-Monday was a very great annual event, and on the previous Sunday evening the new curate was asked to select the hymns to be sung during the next day's march. Among others he thought of a good marching tune, well known to the children (No. 359 in *Hymnal Companion*, where it is called " St. Alban ", and No. 622 in *Church Hymns*, where its title is " Haydn "). But he did not care about the words set to it, and believed that he could substitute better, sitting up very late at night in order to compose them. The next day the children marched round the parish singing, for the first time, the words now familiar in every part of the world:

> Onward, Christian soldiers,
> Marching as to war.

This widespread use of the hymn, however, called for one significant alteration. The Rev. Sabine Baring-Gould had only his Sunday School children in mind when he wrote:

> We are not divided,
> All one body we.

But he felt that these words, unhappily, were in-accurate when the hymn came to be sung far and wide, and so by request a fresh line was substituted for the first of these two, and appears in *Hymns Ancient and Modern* (new edition) thus:

> Though divisions harass,
> All one body we,

thus sacrificing smoothness of rhythm to truth. The popularity of the hymn has been immensely increased since it became wedded to Sir Arthur Sullivan's famous tune "St. Gertrude", a composition for which it is said the author only received a guinea or two, although the firm possessing the copyright must have obtained hundreds of pounds in fees for its use!

## After the Storm

Joseph Addison, who was born in 1672, is well known on account of the important posts he held in the political world, and also from the literary excellence of his essays in the *Spectator*. It was in this paper that there appeared, at various dates, the only five hymns from his pen, of which the best known is probably: "When all Thy Mercies, O my God." Each of these hymns was introduced at the close of an essay, the subject of which it summed up in verse; thus the hymn just mentioned closed an essay on "Gratitude". The hymn of which the first line runs, "How are Thy servants blest, O Lord", owed its inception, however, not so much to the preceding essay as to a personal experience of the writer.

In December, 1700, Addison was on board ship in

the Mediterranean, when the vessel ran into one of the "black storms" sometimes encountered in those waters. So perilous was the condition of the ship, that the captain gave up all as lost, and in preparation for death hastened to confess his sins to a monk who was on board. Addison, however, fortified himself against the terrors of death by a very different and far better preparation, and when eventually the ship escaped the danger that threatened it, his devout thankfulness was expressed some years later in this hymn. It was printed at the close of another essay on "Greatness", and was introduced thus:

"Great painters do not only give us Landskips (note the spelling two hundred years ago) of Gardens, Groves, and Meadows, but very often employ their pencils upon Sea-Pieces. I could wish you could follow their example. If this small sketch may deserve a Place among your Works, I shall accompany it with a Divine Ode, made by a Gentleman upon the conclusion of his Travels"; then follows the hymn:

> How are Thy servants blest, O Lord!
> How sure is their defence!
> Eternal Wisdom is their guide,
> Their help Omnipotence.

The hymn originally consisted of ten verses, one of which has undoubted reference to the deliverance from the storm in the Mediterranean:

> When by the dreadful tempest borne
> High on the broken wave,
> They know Thou art not slow to hear,
> Nor impotent to save.

72

## The Evangelist's Wish

In the summer of 1876, when Mr. Sankey was living at Cohasset, in the State of Massachusetts, he invited Mr. G. C. Needham to stay with him and hold a series of evangelistic meetings. One morning before breakfast, while Mr. Sankey was playing on his organ, Mr. Needham remarked that he wished there were some hymn bearing on the subject of " The Smitten Rock ", as he intended to speak upon it that night. Mr. Sankey replied, as he played, " Here is a new tune which came to me in the night while I slept, and I believe came from the Lord. I want words for it. Why don't you write a hymn for it on your subject?" Mr. Needham objected that he could not write a hymn, and did not understand music sufficiently to fit a hymn to Mr. Sankey's tune, but the great singer, still playing on, only said, " There are pen and paper on that table; try your hand at it; it's a good tune, and I want the words for it."

Mr. Needham says that he at once sat down, and after praying for God's help in his task, wrote the hymn exactly as it was afterwards published. Mr. Sankey took the paper, with the ink barely dry, and sang the hymn through, neither words nor music requiring any alteration, upon which the singer remarked, " I think the Lord gave you the words as truly as He gave me the tune." They then knelt in prayer, asking that the blessing of the Lord might rest upon the hymn and its tune, both being used for the first time that evening. The first verse runs thus :

From the riven Rock there floweth
  Living water, ever clear;
Weary pilgrim, journeying onward,
  Know you not that Fount is near?

    Jesus is the Rock of Ages;
      Smitten, stricken, lo! He dies!
    From His Side a living Fountain,
      Know you not it satisfies?

## *The Search for Manx Music*

Mr. W. H. Gill was an official in the General Post Office, a painter and a student of Manx music. It was this latter hobby which led to the writing of his beautiful hymn for the " Harvest of the Sea ", which supplies a real need in many fishing villages and towns. Mr. Gill's account of its origin, given in 1905, is as follows:

" This hymn was directly inspired by my quest some ten years ago, for Manx music. Among many interesting finds of our once lost national music was a remnant of melody which had once been associated with Manx words. That melody I converted into a hymn tune.

" Then I sought inspiration for a suitable subject. This was found in the occupation of the fisher-folk and the petition in the Manx Book of Common Prayer: ' That it may please Thee to preserve to our use the kindly fruits of the earth, and to continue and restore unto us the blessings of the sea, so as in due time we may enjoy them.' Hence the hymn and its tune, which I devoutly hope may never be divorced." The first line of the hymn is " Hear us,

HYMNS ARISING FROM CIRCUMSTANCES

O Lord, from Heaven, Thy dwelling-place," and the
two verses which refer to the " Harvest of the Sea "
are as follows :

> Our wives, our children we commend to Thee;
>> For them we plough the land and plough the deep;
>> For them by day the golden corn we reap,
> By night the silver harvest of the sea.

> We thank Thee, Lord, for sunshine, dew and rain,
>> Broadcast from Heaven by Thine Almighty Hand—
>> Source of all life, unnumbered as the sand—
> Bird, beast, and fish, fruit, and golden grain.

The tune arranged by Mr. Gill bears the appropriate
name of " Peel Castle ".

## The Sleepless Night

In the *Church Parochial Mission Book* is a striking
hymn by the Rev. Canon W. Hay Aitken, which has
been much used in mission work, and which begins :

> O leave we all for Jesus—
>> The world that fades away,
> The flesh with its wild passions,
>> And Satan's tyrant sway;
> We leave it all for Jesus,
>> Nor will we count it loss;
> For who the fine gold gaining,
>> Will grudge to lose the dross?

At the time of its being written Canon Aitken was
the young Vicar of Christ Church, Everton, Liverpool,
when he received an urgent call from his father, the
Rev. Robert Aitken, to come to his help in a notable
mission which he was conducting at St. Paul's, New-

port. Having a large number of candidates for Confirmation under preparation, young Aitken was naturally unwilling to leave his own parish at the moment, but his father's summons was so imperative that he had no option but to respond.

On reaching Newport his father made him occupy the pulpit in his place that evening, much against his son's will, as he felt that his father was likely to be of more help to the people. On retiring to rest that night, the double burden of the responsibility of the mission and that of his own confirmees away in Liverpool so pressed upon Mr. Aitken that he found it impossible to sleep. He finally gave up the attempt, rose from bed, struck a light, and, sitting down, composed this hymn to be sung at the forthcoming Confirmation in his own parish.

## The Niggardly Congregation

The poet Wordsworth had a nephew, the Rev. Christopher Wordsworth—afterwards Bishop of Lincoln—whose first and only parochial charge was a little country living in Berkshire, with the curious name of Stanford-in-the-Vale-cum-Goosey. The new vicar was much troubled on finding that the villagers had never been taught the duty and privilege of giving; their idea of religion was to receive all the Church doles, in the shape of coal, soup, blankets, etc., and to give nothing.

Mr. Wordsworth was himself a poet of no mean order, a talent which he had probably inherited, and

76

he decided that the best way to teach his parishioners the duty of giving to God was to write a hymn inculcating this lesson and to have it sung in church at intervals of about a month. This method proved much more effective than sermons on "giving" would probably have been, and in time many of his people became really generous givers.

It is, therefore, to this "niggardly congregation" that the Church owes the beautiful hymn which, when published, Wordsworth entitled "Charitable Collections", and which begins,

> O Lord of heaven, and earth, and sea,
> To Thee all praise and glory be;
> How shall we show our love to Thee,
> Giver of all?

The seventh verse generally appears as,

> We *lose* what on ourselves we spend;
> We *have* as treasures without end
> Whatever, Lord, to Thee we lend,
> Who givest all.

But in a number of the newer editions of the older hymn-books, and in the entirely new collections of hymns, verse eight is omitted. It ran thus:

> Whatever, Lord, we lend to Thee
> Repaid a thousandfold will be;
> Then gladly will we give to Thee,
> Giver of all.

## Becalmed at Sea

In June, 1833, a little sailing vessel, bound to Marseilles with a cargo of oranges, lay becalmed for a whole week in the Strait of Bonifacio between the islands of Corsica and Sardinia. On board was a young Oxford clergyman, who had been on a visit to Italy, where he had been taken ill, and now on his recovery was most anxious to get home to England. During that week of waiting John Henry Newman occupied the time, he tells us, by writing verses, three of which—written on the 16th day of June—have become one of the most famous of hymns, and have been described as " one of the finest lyrics of the nineteenth century ". They begin,

> Lead, kindly Light, amid the encircling gloom,
> Lead Thou me on.

When some years ago in America it was decided to hold a Parliament of Religions at Chicago, hymn-books were ransacked to find a hymn which could be sung by everybody, whether Protestants, Roman Catholics, Jews, Mohammedans, or Heathen, and it was decided to sing Newman's hymn at the opening of each day's proceedings.

The common belief is that these lines refer to the question supposed to be then agitating Newman's mind as to whether he should leave the English for the Roman Church. But this idea is quite erroneous, since it was twelve years later when he took this step.

He himself has told us what were the feelings

which gave birth to this prayer for guidance: grief and anger at the condition of the Church which he loved; passionate longing for home and friends; his own weakness and suffering from his late illness, and, above all, his confidence that he had a mission, a work to do, yet not knowing what that work was or where it was to be done—from such mingled emotions sprang this impassioned and pathetic prayer for guidance, based probably on the remembrance of the Pillar of Fire and Cloud which guided the Israelites on their journey to the Promised Land.

## The Silenced Blasphemer

The Rev. Charles Wesley records in his *Journal* that in 1744 he was preaching in Cornwall, in the small church of Laneast. During the sermon, in which he was denouncing the drunken habits of the people and urging them to repentance, a man who was in the congregation began to blaspheme and to contradict the preacher. Upon this Wesley exclaimed, " Who is he that pleads for the devil?" and, upon the blasphemer standing up, he exposed his sin with such tremendous power that the man was driven out of the church. These circumstances suggested to Wesley the writing of the hymn beginning,

Jesus! the Name high over all.
In hell, or earth, or sky,
Angels and men before it fall.
And devils fear and fly.

79

## The Tune that Wanted Words

Mrs. Van Alstyne, better known by her maiden name of Fanny J. Crosby, was the authoress of many beautiful hymns, but the occasion of her writing the most popular of all was not a little curious. She was sitting one day in a room in New York, in conversation with a friend, when Mr. W. H. Doane came in and said to her that he had written a tune and he wanted her to write some words for it.

Mrs. Van Alstyne, who had been blind from the age of six weeks, replied: "Let me hear how the tune goes ".

There was a small organ at hand on which Mr. Doane played the melody to her, when she at once exclaimed, "Why, that tune says ' Safe in the arms of Jesus '; I will see what I can do." She then retired to another room, where she remained alone for some half-hour, and on her return repeated to Mr. Doane the words of the hymn, the best known of all her compositions, and sung the world over:

> Safe in the Arms of Jesus,
> Safe on His gentle Breast;
> There, by His love o'ershaded,
> Sweetly my soul shall rest.

## The Enquiring Children

A fine Ascension hymn owes its origin to the conversation between a gentleman and his children. The latter complained to their father that there was no suitable hymn known to them for Ascension Day, and also questioned him as to what the feelings of the disciples had been when they saw the cloud receive their Lord out of their sight. The gentleman, who was a friend of Dean Stanley, mentioned this conversation to him, and thus inspired the Dean to write one of our most beautiful Ascension hymns, beginning,

> He is gone—A cloud of light
> Has received Him from our sight.

The original hymn consisted of seven verses of eight lines each, which was obviously too long for use in public worship, so that the Dean's first verse, commencing "He is gone—beyond the skies," as well as others, are usually omitted. The greater part of the hymn is devoted to answering the children's question, and beautifully describes the disciples' feelings after the Ascension of their Lord, as in the following verse:

> He is gone—We heard Him say,
>   "Good that I should go away."
> Gone is that dear Form and Face,
> But not gone His present grace;
> Though Himself no more we see,
> Comfortless we cannot be;
> No, His Spirit still is ours,
> Quickening, freshening all our powers.

## From the Pilgrim's Progress

One morning in the year 1865 Mrs. Ellen H. Gates — the authoress of "If you cannot on the ocean," the hymn which appealed so strongly to President Abraham Lincoln—received a letter from Mr. Philip

Phillips, asking her to write an appropriate hymn based upon this enclosed extract from Bunyan's *Pilgrim's Progress*:

"Now I saw in my dream that these two men went in at the gate; and lo, as they entered, they were transfigured; and they had raiment put on them that shone like gold. There were also those that met them with harps and crowns, and gave to them; the harps to praise withal, and the crowns in token of honour. Then I heard in my dream that all the bells in the city rang again for joy, and that it was said unto them: 'Enter ye into the joy of our Lord!' Now, just as the gates were opened to let in the men, I looked in after them, and behold the city shone like the sun; the streets also were paved with gold; and in them walked many men, with crowns on their heads and palms in their hands, and golden harps to sing praises withal. After that, they shut up the gates, which, when I had seen, I wished myself among them."

Obediently to Mr. Phillips' request, Mrs. Gates wrote the hymn which begins,

> I will sing you a song of that beautiful land,
>   The far-away home of the soul;
> Where no storms ever beat on the glittering strand,
>   While the years of eternity roll.

When Mr. Phillips received the verse he sat down, with his little boy upon his knee, and read once more those closing scenes in Bunyan's immortal story; then he turned to his organ and wrote for the hymn the tune which appears under his name in *Sacred Songs and Solos,* No. 114.[1] Mr. Phillips says that the hymn seems to have been specially blessed by God to the comfort of many souls. One man told him that he had joined in the singing of it at no less than one hundred and twenty funerals. "And", says Mr. Phillips, "it was sung at the funeral of my own dear boy, who had sat on my knee when I wrote the tune."

## The Singer's Request

When William O. Cushing was living in Moravia, New York, in the year 1876, he received one day a letter from Mr. Sankey, the Gospel singer and evangelist, containing the request, "Send me something to help me in my Gospel work." Mr. Cushing looked upon such a demand as a direct call from God, and prayed earnestly that He would give him something to write which should be to His glory. While thus waiting upon God, a new hymn began to form itself in his mind, "the outcome", says Mr. Cushing, "of many tears, many heart-conflicts and soul-yearnings, of which the world can know nothing." Thus it ran:

> Oh, safe to the Rock that is higher than I,
> My soul in its conflicts and sorrows would fly;
> So sinful, so weary, Thine own would I be;
> Thou Blest "Rock of Ages", I'm hiding in Thee.

## The Absent Sister

In November, 1865, Miss Frances Ridley Havergal

[1] *The collection of 750 pieces.*

was a visitor at Shareshill Parsonage, when she received a letter from one of her nieces who was at boarding-school. The girl was very much depressed in spirit; she was feeling very tired and weary with her work, she was oppressed with loneliness and, to crown all this, the rejoicings over her brother's coming-of-age had just taken place and she was unable to leave school in order to be present. So she wrote to her aunt, pouring out her feelings to her, and from her letter came the suggestion for one of Miss Havergal's hymns, not very well known, but very beautiful. The first verse is as follows:

> Yes! He knows the way is dreary,
>   Knows the weakness of our frame,
> Knows that hand and heart are weary;
>   He, " in all points ", felt the same.
> He is near to help and bless;
> Be not weary, onward press.

## The Dying Lady's Request

The poet, James Montgomery, returned home to Sheffield, on May 24, 1832, from Bristol, in which city he had been attending some religious meetings. No sooner had he entered his house than an album was put into his hand, which had been sent to him by a London lady. She had been for a long time a great admirer of Montgomery's poems and hymns, and was now on her death-bed, but could not repress her intense desire to see his handwriting in her book. Montgomery was touched by this wish of the dying woman, and inscribed in her album the hymn begin-

84

ning. " I cannot call affliction sweet ", which, although not widely known, has found a place in several modern hymnals. The first and last stanzas are as follows:

> I cannot call affliction sweet,
>   And yet 'twas good to bear;
> Affliction brought me to Thy feet,
>   And I found comfort there.

> Lord, grant me grace for every day,
>   Whate'er my state may be,
> Through life, in death, with truth to say,
>   " My God is all to me!"

## The Larger Room

The Rev. John Newton, in 1764, became curate-in-charge of Olney in Buckinghamshire. Formerly an atheist and at one time captain of a slave-ship, he became converted to God, and was eventually ordained by the Bishop of Lincoln.

At Olney he did a wonderful work for God, and during each week he held regularly no less than four meetings for prayer, two on Sunday (at 6 a.m. and 8 p.m.) and two on Tuesday (at 5 a.m. and at night). This latter, on Tuesday evenings, was the largest of all his weekly gatherings, and eventually it outgrew the place of meeting.

In April, 1769, Mr. Newton, writing to a friend, says: "We are going to remove our prayer meeting to the great room in the Great House. It is a noble place, with a parlour behind it, and holds one hundred and thirty people conveniently. Pray for us, that the Lord may be in the midst of us there, and that as He has now given us a Rehoboth (with reference to Gen. 26: 22), and has made room for us, so He may be pleased to add to our numbers, and make us fruitful in the land."

One of Newton's little devices for keeping up his people's interest in their prayer meetings as the provision of a new hymn every Tuesday evening, which he often used as a text for his address; these were sometimes written by himself, and sometimes by his friend the poet Cowper, then a resident at Olney. For this momentous occasion of the removal to the larger room, two special hymns were written; one was by Newton himself beginning, " O Lord, our languid souls inspire," but which we know best in its modern form, which begins " Great Shepherd of Thy people, hear "; the other hymn, by Cowper, was the well-known " Jesus, where'er Thy people meet." When these circumstances are known, the words of several lines in both hymns are seen to have special reference to the occasion. In Newton's hymn we have the lines:

> As Thou has given a place for prayer,
> So give us hearts to pray;

and again :

> Within these walls let holy peace,
> And love, and concord, dwell.

Cowper's hymn has a clear reference to the change

from the old place of gathering to the new in the lines:

> Dear Shepherd of Thy chosen few,
> Thy former mercies here renew;

while one of his stanzas has two of its lines so limited in its reference to the special circumstances as to cause its omission from the hymn as we know it, viz:

> Come Thou and fill this wider space,
> And bless us with a large increase.

# Chapter 5

HYMNS SUGGESTED BY SURROUNDINGS

## *The Women in the Field*

It was in the month of February, 1832, that James Montgomery, the well-known hymn writer and a blind friend, Rowland Hodgson, were returning from Bath in a carriage. On the road between Gloucester and Tewkesbury they passed a field to which Montgomery's attention was attracted. Evidently it had been recently ploughed and harrowed, as the surface was level and not furrowed, and in it were working a number of women and girls in rows one behind the other. From their stooping attitude they might have been weeding, had not the clean fresh surface of the field proved this to be impossible, and it seemed to Montgomery that they must be planting something, although they were too far off for him to see very clearly.

Turning to his blind friend, Montgomery described the scene to him, and he at once replied: " Oh, I dare say it is dibbling, a much more economical way of sowing than the usual method. Holes are made in the field, and two or three grains of corn dropped into each hole." " Well, give me broadcast sowing," rejoined Montgomery, " for this dibbling is most un-picturesque, with grace neither of attitude nor of motion in it."

As the carriage rolled on its way, Montgomery's thoughts ran upon the subject of husbandry, until, he says, they began to turn into verse, and in the course of the next few miles they had assumed the form of the seven stanzas of one of his widely used hymns, beginning,

> Sow in the morn thy seed,
>   At eve hold not thine hand;
> To doubt and fear give thou no heed,
>   Broadcast it o'er the land.

The hymn was headed " The Field of the World ", and was printed for the use of the Sheffield Sunday School Union among their Whitsuntide hymns the same year. It will be observed that the poet in his first verse adheres to his preference for " broadcasting " rather than " dibbling " as a method of sowing.

## The Words on the Tombstone

A friend of Mrs. Margaret Mackay was driving her one day through the beautiful roads and lanes of Devonshire. Passing a country churchyard the ladies were attracted by its appearance, and, pulling up the pony carriage, went in to look at the graves.

The churchyard was not laid out as a garden, but it was well cared for, and the grass was of a lovely green. " It was ", says Mrs. Mackay, " a place of such sweet, entire repose as to leave a lasting impression on the memory." As the friends strolled on they came to a headstone, on which were carved the three words "Sleeping in Jesus", words which, seen amid such beautiful and peaceful surroundings, fastened themselves on Mrs. Mackay's mind.

On their arrival home, Mrs. Mackay at once took pencil and paper, and began to write that touching hymn, which has not only been so widely sung, but has itself often furnished words for many other tombstones, beginning.

> Asleep in Jesus! Blessed sleep,
> From which none ever wake to weep;
> A calm and undisturbed repose,
> Unbroken by the last of foes.

The influence of the quiet and peaceful spot, where the suggestion for the hymn was given, is clearly traceable in Mrs. Mackay's delightful lines.


## The Cancelled Removal

In 1772 the Rev. John Fawcett, then pastor of the Baptist Chapel at Wainsgate, near Hebden Bridge, in Yorkshire, received and accepted an invitation to succeed the famous Dr. J. Gill as minister of Carter's Lane Chapel, London. The farewell sermon at Wainsgate was preached on the Sunday, and was followed by the arrival of the waggons for removal. On these the pastor's furniture and household effects were packed, and all was ready for departure, when at that last moment the affection and the tearful pleadings of his flock gained the day and Mr. Fawcett decided to cancel his acceptance of the great London pastorate, and to remain in his little village of Wainsgate, where he continued to minister until, five years later, a new chapel was built for him at Hebden Bridge. It was this touching incident which inspired him to write the well-known hymn, which opens thus:

> Blest be the tie that binds
>   Our hearts in Christian love;
> The fellowship of kindred minds
>   Is like to that above.

## The Blast Furnaces

At one period of his life Charles Wesley preached with marvellous success to the colliers of Newcastle, which, as usual with him, called forth his thankfulness in hymns, four of which were then written. One of these undoubtedly has the imagery of the first verse suggested by the blast furnaces and burning pit-heaps which are scattered over the district around Newcastle, and which at night illumine the whole neighbourhood. The verse runs:

> See how great a flame aspires,
>   Kindled by a spark of grace!
> Jesu's love the nations fires,
>   Sets the kingdoms on a blaze;
> To bring fire on earth He came,
>   Kindled in some hearts it is,
> Oh, that all might catch the flame,
>   All partake the glorious bliss!

## The Walk Round the Cathedral

On Whitsun-Tuesday, June 14, 1870, the Ninth Festival of the Canterbury Diocesan Choral Union was held in the cathedral, the music being rendered by nine hundred voices. After it was over Dean Alford arranged that at the next festival, Whitsun-Tuesday, 1871, a processional hymn should be sung for which he had furnished both words and music.

The Dean was already well known as a hymn-writer, although his work has been criticized as " cold and conventional ", containing neither striking poetry nor original thought. Be that as it may, there can be no question as to the popularity of his hymn, " Come, ye thankful people, come," nor of the real beauty of " Ten thousand times ten thousand "; while his hymn " In token that thou shalt not fear," first used at the Baptism of his own first child in Wymeswold Church, occurs in a greater number of hymn-books than any other hymn for use at that Sacrament, although its poetical merit is not very great.

Previously to the festival in 1870, the precentor of Canterbury Cathedral had requested the Dean to write a processional hymn, but on receiving the composition he ventured to point out that, although the hymn was good in some ways, it was quite unsuitable for singing while marching in a procession. He then suggested that the Dean should walk slowly round the cathedral, following the course that a procession would take, and compose another hymn as he walked. The Dean adopted this advice, and walked round the cathedral, composing as he went, after which he handed the precentor his new hymn, beginning.

> Forward be our watchword,
> Steps and voices joined.

The second of the above lines would seem to indictate that the precentor's hint was still uppermost in his mind, since it was the disunion of " steps and voices " which had marred his first hymn, while the surroundings of the majestic cathedral, amid which he was walking, have left their unmistakable imprint upon the fifth verse:

> Into God's high temple
> > Onward as we press,
> Beauty spreads around us,
> > Born of holiness.
> Arch, and vault, and carving,
> > Lights of varied tone,
> Softened words and holy,
> > Prayer and praise alone.

Of the tune for this hymn the Dean, curiously enough, wrote the treble and bass, while Miss Lindsay (afterwards Mrs. Worthington Bliss) added the two inner parts. But his anticipation of hearing his verses sung at the next great Choral Festival was never realized, for he died six months before the following Whitsuntide. It was the Dean's last hymn.

## The Earthquake

There was a most alarming earthquake in London on February 8, 1750, which caused widespread terror and alarm. Four weeks later followed a still more severe shock, the people rushing from their houses into Hyde Park, Moorfields, and other open spaces, for safety, while the excitement was increased by a mad dragoon, who declared that all London would be swallowed up on the 4th of April following.

When the second shock occurred at 5 a.m. Charles Wesley was just giving out his text at an early service in the Foundry Chapel, which he at once changed for the words " Therefore will we not fear, though the earth be moved, and the hills be carried into the midst of the sea " (Psa. 66 : 2, Prayer Book Version). The general fear and alarm gave a marvellous opportunity for Whitefield and Wesley to preach the Gospel to the people, crowds of whom flocked to them from every quarter, the chapel being filled even at midnight. On this occasion Charles Wesley composed no less than nineteen hymns, suitable for the time. The following verse, quoted from one of them beginning " How weak the thoughts, and vain ", will show how he made use of the earthquake.

> A house we call our own,
>   Which cannot be o'erthrown;
> In the general ruin sure
>   Storms and earthquakes it defies
> Built immovably secure,
>   Built eternal in the skies.

## A Hymn from a Hymn

Few hymns have so " caught on " in children's meetings as Mr. Bliss's beautifully simple lines, beginning,

I am so glad that our Father in heaven
Tells of His love in the Book He has given;
Wonderful things in the Bible I see,
This is the dearest, that Jesus loves me.

The hymn really originated from another, which had the chorus " Oh, how I love Jesus!" Mr. Bliss was present at a meeting in which he had joined over and over again in singing this chorus, when, he says, the thought came to him that while he had been thus singing about his poor love for Christ he ought rather to sing about Christ's great love for him. Under the influence of this thought he went back to his home, and there wrote this most attractive and beautiful children's hymn.

## In the Cleft of the Rock

The Rev. Augustus M. Toplady, when Vicar of Blagdon, in Somersetshire, was walking through Burrington Combe, a beautiful spot some two or three miles from his home, when he was caught in a sudden storm. The particular place is very exposed, affording no shelter, but Toplady espied a cleft running down a mass of rock beside the road, in which he was able to take refuge until the storm abated (see the Frontispiece).

A man of saintly character, his thoughts were turned by the incident to spiritual things, and picking up a playing card which he found lying on the ground at his feet, he wrote upon the back of it the hymn of which it has been said that " no other

English hymn can be named which has laid so broad and firm a grasp upon the English-speaking world ", beginning,

> Rock of Ages! cleft for me!
> Let me hide myself in Thee!

The playing card upon which the hymn was first written is still preserved in America.

It was this hymn which afforded such comfort, among multitudes of others, to the Prince Consort and which he repeated constantly upon his death-bed. " For," said he, " if in this hour I had only my worldly honours and dignities to depend upon, I should be poor indeed!"

## The Collapse of the Floor

On March 14, 1744, Charles Wesley paid his third visit to Leeds, and a great meeting of the members of the Society was held in an old upper room, which was crowded out, numbers being unable to obtain admission. Suddenly the rafters supporting the floor broke off close to the main beam, the floor collapsed, and over a hundred people were precipitated into the room below. Mercifully none were killed, though some were severely injured, Wesley himself escaping with but slight injuries.

He relates that he saw the people under him, lying in heaps, and cried out, " Fear not! The Lord is with us; our lives are all safe ", and immediately gave out the Doxology, "Praise God, from Whom all blessings flow."

It was after this escape that Wesley wrote the hymn of twelve verses which began "Glory and thanks to God we give," and was headed "After a Deliverance from Death by the Fall of a House." The hymn in its original form was unsuited for congregational use, but six of its verses form a fairly well-known hymn, opening thus,

> The great Archangel's trump shall sound,

which appears in Wesley's Hymns under the title "Describing Judgment." It displays a great power of word-painting, as can be seen from the following verses, which are obviously framed upon Wesley's thrilling remembrance of gazing down upon the mass of injured after the floor had given way:

> The earth, and all the works therein,
>     Dissolve, by raging flames destroyed,
> While we survey the awful scene,
>     And mount above the fiery void.
>
> By faith we now transcend the skies,
>     And on that ruined world look down;
> By love above all height we rise,
>     And share the everlasting throne.

## The Drive to the Shops

In the middle of last century some little Irish boys were complaining to each other that the Church Catechism, which they had to learn, was dreadfully dull and dreary. Their godmother overheard their remarks, and set herself each week to write verses which should make the meaning of the Catechism plain, until presently the boys became full of interest in the subject.

These hymns have been sung, and are beloved, by thousands of children ever since: such as " Do no sinful action ", written to explain the Baptismal promise to " renounce the devil and all his works "; " All things bright and beautiful ", expanding the truth of " I believe in God the Father Almighty, Maker of heaven and earth "; " Once in royal David's city ", drawn from the words " And in Jesus Christ, His Only Son, our Lord, Who was conceived by the Holy Ghost, born of the Virgin Mary," etc.

The most famous of them all, perhaps, had its first verse suggested by the fact that the lady in question, Mrs. Alexander, had to drive in to the city of Derry on her shopping expeditions, a city which is still surrounded by its old walls. By the side of the road, close to the city, was a little grass covered hill, which always reminded Mrs. Alexander of Calvary. When, therefore, she came to expound for her little godsons the words " Suffered under Pontius Pilate, was crucified dead, and buried," this well-known spot came into her mind, and so she wrote:

> There is a green hill far away,
>   Without a city wall,
> Where the dear Lord was crucified,
>   Who died to save us all.

It may be of interest, however, to recall the fact

that, despite the many wonderful pictures of the world's greatest tragedy representing Calvary as Mrs. Alexander imagined it, there is no statement in Scripture to the effect that our Lord was crucified on a " hill ", any more than there can be found the name " Calvary " in the Gospel narrative. All four evangelists simply speak of the scene of the Crucifixion as a " place ", while " Calvary " is simply the Latinizing of St. Luke's word which he uses when he tells us that the " place " was called " The Skull "— as a glance at Luke 23: v. 33 in the Revised Version will show. It is true that the name *may* have been given from the place being a small, rounded eminence, in shape like a human head, but this is merely conjecture and not certainty.

## In Hiding on the River Bank

The Rev. David Nelson, although an ordained minister, owned at one time a plantation and slaves in America, until one day he heard an address on the subject which completely altered his views. He disposed of his plantation, declaring that he would live on potatoes and salt rather than own slaves, and his bold denunciation of the practice brought down upon him the wrath of his slave-owning neighbours.

He was driven from his home, and hunted for three days and nights through the woods and swamps, until he emerged on the bank of the Mississippi River. He managed to communicate his whereabouts by signs to friends on the opposite bank of the great stream, and then concealed himself in the bushes until nightfall, hearing all around him the voices of his pursuers, who even thrust their guns into the very clump of bushes in which he lay hidden, but failed to discover him.

Lying there, driven from home, gazing at the swiftly gliding waters and at the land of safety beyond, he composed, and wrote on the back of a letter which chanced to be in his pocket, the hymn beginning,

> My days are gliding swiftly by,
>     And I, a pilgrim stranger,
> Would not detain them as they fly,
>     Those hours of toil and danger;
> For oh, we stand on Jordan's strand,
>     Our friends are passing over;
> And, just before, the shining shore
>     We may almost discover.

As the evening drew on some members of the Church at Quincy, on the opposite bank, crossed over in a canoe, under the pretence of fishing, and, meeting him as he rushed down to the water's edge, conveyed him to safety.

Chapter 6

## *The Terrible Affliction of Insanity*

To lose one's reason is surely the most awful affliction that can be endured by any human being. Yet
from such a terrible experience the Church of God
has gained one of her most wonderful hymns. The
poet Cowper was a deeply religious man, but became
insane for a time in 1773, in October of which year
he attempted to commit suicide by drowning in the
River Ouse at Olney, in Buckinghamshire.

His friend, the Rev. John Newton, Vicar of Olney,
has pointed out that even this attempt was a proof of
his perfect submission to the will of God; for, he
says, " it was solely owing to the power the enemy
had of impressing upon his disturbed imagination that
it was the will of God he should, after the example of
Abraham, perform an expensive act of obedience, and
offer, not a son, but himself."

Some believe that it was early in 1773—in " the
twilight of departing reason " as one writer describes
it—while others think it was *after* his insanity had

101

left him, in 1774, that he wrote the hymn beginning
" God moves in a mysterious way His wonders to
perform "— a hymn which has become one of the
most widely known in English-speaking countries.

How truly pathetic, in the light of this terrible affliction, are the lines in which the writer undoubtedly
refers to his own awful experience, in words which
breathe the deepest submission and trust:

> Ye fearful saints, fresh courage take;
>     The clouds ye so much dread
> Are big with mercy, and shall break
>     In blessings on your head.
>
> Judge not the Lord by feeble sense,
>     But trust Him for His grace;
> Behind a frowning providence
>     He hides a smiling face.

## The Sick Friend

In the Church of Holy Trinity, Ripon, of which the
author of this volume is Vicar, is a tablet with an
inscription:

> TO THE MEMORY OF SUSANNAH POWLEY,
>         ONLY DAUGHTER
> OF MRS. UNWIN, THE FRIEND OF COWPER.

The friendship between the poet and Mrs. Unwin
was true and deep, and to that friendship is due one
of the most tender and touching hymns we possess.
In December, 1769, Mrs. Unwin was very seriously
ill, and in a letter to another friend Cowper writes

of his great distress and anxiety concerning one whom he calls "the chief of blessing I have met with in my journey". With touching resignation he adds: "Her illness has been a sharp trial to me. Oh! that it may have a sanctified effect, that I may rejoice to surrender up to the Lord my dearest comforts the moment He shall require them. Oh, for no will but the will of my Heavenly Father!"

He then thanks the friend for some verses sent to him, and encloses some of his own in return, these being those beautiful lines so well known throughout the Christian Church:

> Oh, for a closer walk with God,
> A calm and heavenly frame,
> A light to shine upon the road
> That leads me to the Lamb.

Cowper's own account of their composition is as follows: "I began to compose them yesterday morning (December 9, 1769) before daybreak, but fell asleep at the end of the first two lines; when I awaked again, the third and fourth verses were whispered to my heart in a way which I have often experienced."

Truly does a writer say of these wonderful verses, and of the light which Cowper's letter throws upon them: "We read a new and pathetically personal history and meaning in the earnest and throbbing lines, and are brought face to face with an agony which would have been voiceless but for the mercy and goodness of God."

## The Repentant Author

The famous hymn writer, James Montgomery, at one time wrote and printed in the paper of which he was editor, *The Sheffield Iris,* a series of essays entitled " The Whisperer, or Hints and Speculations by Gabriel Silvertongue, Gent." These essays, afterwards reproduced in volume form, were full of irreverent references to and quotations from Holy Scripture. Some ten years later, the author saw his wrongdoing, and repented. He destroyed all the copies of his book which he could find, and expressed his repentance in the hymn which he then wrote, beginning " I left the God of truth and light."

The two opening verses run thus:

> I left the God of truth and light,
>   I left the God Who gave me breath,
> To wander in the wilds of night,
>   And perish in the snares of death.
>
> Sweet was His Service, and His yoke
>   Was light, and easy to be borne;
> Through all His bands of love I broke,
>   I cast away His gifts with scorn.

The two closing stanzas are as follows:

> My suffering, slain, and risen Lord,
>   In sore distress I turn to Thee;
> I claim acceptance on Thy word,
>   My God! my God forsake not me.
>
> Prostrate before the mercy seat,
>   I dare not, if I would, despair;
> None ever perished at Thy feet,
>   And I will lie for ever there.

# After his Last Sermon

The Rev. Henry Lyte, the author of the world-famous hymn, beginning:

Abide with me; fast falls the eventide,

was Vicar of Lower Brixham, in Devonshire. In the year 1847, at the age of fifty-four, he felt the approach of life's eventide, and his rapidly failing health determined him to spend the winter in Italy. It was as the date of his departure drew near that from his couch he gave to the world this magnificent hymn, which has found a place in almost every hymnal. His daughter has given the following account of the day of its composition:

" The summer was passing away, and the month of September (that month in which he was once more to quit his native land) arrived, and each day seemed to have a special value as being one day nearer his departure. His family were surprised, and almost alarmed, at his announcing his intention of preaching once more to his people. His weakness, and the possible danger attending the effort, were urged to prevent it, but in vain. He felt that he should be enabled to fulfil his wish, and feared not for the result.

" His expectation was well founded. He did preach, and amid the breathless attention of his hearers gave them a sermon on the Holy Communion. He afterwards assisted in the administration of the Holy Eucharist, and thought necessarily much exhausted by the exertion and excitement of this effort, yet his friends had no reason to believe it had been hurtful to him.

" In the evening of the same day he placed in the hands of a near and dear relative the little hymn ' Abide with me ', with an air of his own composing, adapted to the words."

This took place on September 4th, and Henry Lyte died at Nice on the 20th of the following November, his last words being " Peace! Joy!"

## The Apologetic Hymn

Phoebe Brown was born in America in 1783, and left an orphan at two years of age. Seven years later she fell into the hands of a relative who kept a county gaol, and her son records that the tale of the next nine years " is a narrative of such deprivations, cruel treatment, and toil as breaks my heart to read ".

At the age of eighteen she escaped from this bondage, and was sent by some kind people to school for three months, which was apparently her sole education. Even after marriage her life was one of poverty and trial. Her son, the Rev. S. R. Brown, D.D., became the first American missionary to Japan, and, despite all her own disadvantages, her hymns are said to be superior to those of any other female writer of hymns in America at that time. One of the most popular of these hymns is the one now beginning " I love to steal awhile away," and a few hymns, it has been truly said, have a more pathetic history.

106

Mrs. Brown was living at Ellington with, as she says, " four little children, in a small unfurnished house, a sick sister in the only finished room, and not a place above or below where I could retire for devotion ". Not far off stood the finest house in the neighbourhood, with a large garden. Towards this the poor woman used to walk at dusk, delighting " to smell the fragrance of the fruits and flowers, though she could not see them ", and to hold communion with nature and with God. In doing this she never dreamed that she was intruding, or that she was being watched and her motives misconstrued, until one day that lady of the mansion approached her, and with great rudeness said :

" Mrs. Brown, why do you come up at evening so near our house, and then go back without coming in? If you want anything, why don't you come in and ask for it?"

Mrs. Brown writes : " There was something in her manner, more than her words, which grieved me. I went home, and that evening was left alone. After my children were all in bed, except my baby, I sat down in the kitchen with my child in my arms, when the grief of my heart burst forth in a flood of tears. I took pen and paper and gave vent to my oppressed heart."

The poem thus written is headed " An Apology for my Twilight Rambles, Addressed to a Lady, August, 1818." The original has been somewhat altered, and the first stanza omitted, in the version of the hymn so popular in America, the first three verses of which run thus :

I love to steal awhile away
　　From every cumbering care,
And spend the hours of closing day
　　In humble, grateful prayer.

I love in solitude to shed
　　The penitential tear,
And all His promises to plead,
　　Where none but God can hear.

I love to think on mercies past,
　　And future good implore;
And all my cares and sorrows cast
　　On Him Whom I adore.

The hymn appears in Sankey's collection (750 pieces), *Sacred Songs and Solos,* No. 634.

## The Great Poet's Last Hymn

It had been said that, taking quantity and quality into consideration, Charles Wesley was the greatest hymn-writer of all ages. His hymns number some 6,500, and though it would be impossible for all to be of equal merit, yet a very large number of these reach the highest standard. On every conceivable occasion he expressed his feelings in a hymn. His conversion, his marriage, the earthquake panic, the rumours of a French invasion, the defeat of Prince Charles Edward at Culloden, the Gordon riots, all the Festivals of the Church, scenes from the Bible, incidents that fell within his own experience, the home calls of his various friends—all these furnished occasions for the exercise of his gift. The last of this magnificent series of contributions to the hymnody of the Church was inspired by the thought of his own approaching death.

At the age of eighty, and in extreme feebleness, he had remained silent and quiet for some time, when he called Mrs. Wesley to him and desired her to write at his dictation his final hymn. Truly has it been said of him that " for fifty years Christ as the Redeemer of men had been the subject of his effective ministry, and his loftiest songs, and he may be said to have died with a hymn to Christ on his lips." Consisting only of a single stanza, the hymn is naturally unsuited for public use, and, therefore, is very little known (although it is included in the *Methodist Hymn Book*), so that it may be of interest to my readers to quote it here in its striking pathos and beauty :

> In age and feebleness extreme,
> Who shall a helpless worm redeem?
> Jesus! my only hope Thou art,
> Strength of my failing flesh and heart;
> Oh, could I catch one smile from Thee,
> And drop into eternity!

## The Shadows of the Poplars

Mary Bachelor was the daughter of a minister, and living with her brother, to whom she was devotedly attached, and who was himself also a minister. All her joys and sorrows were confided to her brother, the selfishness of thus adding to his own cares never occurring to her, until one day when she had been telling him of some special trouble that had come upon her.

She was standing by the open window, looking out upon the lawn, when her conscience reproached her for her thoughtfulness, and as she saw the tall poplar-trees throwing their long shadows across the grass she thought to herself that they represented exactly what she had been doing to her brother, in thrusting upon him the burden of her cares. " Why did I do it?" she thought; "why did I not bury my own sorrows, and try to add brightness to his life?"

Tears of regret were filling her eyes as she left the window and retired to her own little room at the top of the house, and there she wrote the hymn which has borne its message and brought real comfort to many sorrowful and care-laden hearts :

> Go bury thy sorrow,
>   The world hath its share
> Go bury it deeply,
>   Go hide it with care.
> Go think of it calmly,
>   When curtained by night;
> Go tell it to Jesus,
>   And all will be right.

## His Wife's Funeral Sermon

Maxwell Cornelius, when a young man living in Pittsburg , broke his leg, which the doctors had to amputate, thus maiming him for life. This decided him to abandon business and go to college, after which he became a minister. He had charge of a large Presbyterian Church at Pasadena, in California, but had considerable difficulty in clearing the building of debt. A short time after accomplishing this, his wife died. Dr. Cornelius himself preached the funeral sermon, and at the conclusion quoted a hymn which he had composed a short time before, and of which the first verse ran:

> Not now, but in the coming years—
>   It may be in the better land—
> We'll read the meaning of our tears,
>   And there, some time, we'll understand.

Both sermon and hymn were published in a newspaper, and were read by Major Whittle, who was so struck by their beauty that he cut them out and carried them in his Bible for three months, at the end of which time he, one day, wrote for them a chorus:

> Then trust in God through all thy days;
>   Fear not! for He doth hold thy hand;
> Though dark thy way, still sing and praise;
>   Some time, some time we'll understand.

Shortly after writing these lines he handed both hymn and chorus to his friend Mr. McGranahan, to whose music the words are now sung.

## The Marriage Hymn

The hymn in the *Methodist Hymn Book* beginning "Appointed by Thee, we meet in Thy Name," is an abridged form of a hymn by Charles Wesley, of a different significance and with an interesting origin. Wesley had reached the age of forty with no thought of marriage, desiring to give himself wholly to the preaching of the Gospel. But about this time he began to wonder whether he had not been wrong. He met with a young lady in Wales who appealed strongly to his affections, and he consulted his brother (who gave him no help) as well as other friends. He prayed and waited, writing several hymns expressing his feelings during that time. Finally he was married to Miss Sarah Gwynne in a Welsh Church on April 8, 1749, and the hymn referred to is extracted from the marriage hymn from Wesley's pen which was sung on that occasion. The original opening verses of the hymn ran thus:

> How happy the pair Whom Jesus unites
> In friendship to share Angelic delights,
> Whose chaste conversation Is coupled with fear,
> Whose sure expectation Is holiness here.
>
> My Jesus, my Lord, Thy grace I commend,
> So kind to afford My weakness a friend,
> Thy only good pleasure On me hath bestowed
> A heavenly treasure, A servant of God.

## Kept in his Pocket Book

Dr. Ray Palmer began his life as a clerk in a dry-goods store; he ended it as a beloved pastor of the Congregational Church of America, a learned Doctor of Divinity, and a famous hymn writer! Remarkably enough the first of all his hymns is the most widely known and the best loved. From his dry-goods store he had passed to an academy and thence to Yale College, where he took his degree in 1830, being then only twenty-two years of age. On leaving college he took a teaching engagement, and it was then that he wrote his first and finest hymn:

My faith looks up to Thee,
Thou Lamb of Calvary,
    Saviour Divine;
Now hear me while I pray;
Take all my sins away;
Oh, let me from this day
    Be wholly Thine.

The author says, concerning its composition, " I gave form to what I felt, by writing, with little effort, these stanzas. I recollect I wrote them with very tender emotion, and ended the last line with tears ", that last line being,

Oh bear me safe above—
A ransomed soul.

When Mr. Palmer had finished the hymn he placed the manuscript in his pocket-book and carried it about with him for some time, until one day, in Boston, he met Dr. Lowell Mason who was then compiling, in conjunction with Dr. T. Hastings, a new hymn-book, entitled *Spiritual Songs for Social Worship*.

Dr. Mason asked Mr. Palmer whether he had not some hymn to contribute to the new book, whereupon Mr. Palmer pulled out his pocket-book and handed him this manuscript. On reaching home, Dr. Mason was so impressed with the verses that he wrote for it the well-known tune called " Olivet," to which it is usually sung.

Although not at first attracting much notice, the hymn has now made its way into all English-speaking countries, and has also been translated into numerous languages.

Dr. Palmer wrote many other hymns, one, composed
113

twenty-eight years later, again in response to a request for contributions to a new book and accounted by many as the author's second best hymn for merit and beauty, beginning,

> Jesus, these eyes have never seen
> That radiant form of Thine;
> The veil of sense hangs dark between
> Thy Blessed Face and mine,

a hymn which deserves a far wider recognition than it has obtained in this country. But, Dr. Palmer's first hymn still stands pre-eminent among his compositions. The author, in writing to the editor of *The Hymnal Companion,* said of it: " It was introduced into England in 1840, has been translated into other languages, and has been referred to as one of the last hymns that dying saints have sung, or desired to hear. It has been a comfort to Christian hearts, doubtless, chiefly because it expresses in a simple way that act which is most central in all Christian life—the act of trust in the Atoning Lamb." Dr. Mason was a true prophet when, meeting Mr. Palmer in the street soon after he had handed him the hymn, he exclaimed: " Mr. Palmer, you may live many years and do many good things, but I think you will be best known to posterity as the author of ' My faith looks up to Thee.' "

## During the Bazaar

A misconception is frequently uttered in connection with Miss Charlotte Elliott's hymn, beginning,

> Just as I am, without one plea.

That Miss Elliott owed her conversion to the Rev. Dr. Cæsar Malan is undisputed. It is related that he ventured to ask her some question as to her spiritual state which she then deeply resented, but that some weeks later she went to him and told him that she now had the earnest desire to really be a Christian, and asked him to tell her how to come to Christ, adding that she supposed she would first have to try and make herself more worthy of Him, to which Dr. Malan replied : " Come to Him just as you are."

To this experience, naturally enough, has been ascribed the writing of the hymn, the words " Just as I am," which begin every verse, appearing to be the repetition of the truth she learned that day.

Quite possibly the words of Dr. Malan did recur to her, and so become the refrain of the hymn, but the actual occasion of its writing was very different, as related by Dr. Moule, the late Bishop of Durham, a relative of the Elliott family.

Miss Elliott's brother, the Rev. H. V. Elliott, was planning the erection of St. Mary's Hall at Brighton, as a school for the daughters of clergymen, and it was decided to hold a bazaar in aid of the fund.

Miss Elliott was then forty-five years of age and suffering from ill-health, so that while " Westfield Lodge ", her home at Brighton, was all astir with preparations for the bazaar, Miss Elliott herself could do nothing. The night before the event the thought of her uselessness kept her awake in sorrow, until she began to question the reality of the whole of her own spiritual life.

The next day, the busy day of the bazaar, when all the rest of the family were gone, leaving Miss Elliott lying on the sofa in great weakness, these doubts and fears returned with fresh force, and she felt that she must fight out this battle once for all.

Gathering up, therefore, the great truths which were the foundation of her faith—her Lord, His love, His power, His promises—she took pen and paper from the table, and set down, as the definite expression of her hope of salvation and for her own comfort, those wonderful lines, beginning,

> Just as I am, without one plea,
> But that Thy Blood was shed for me,
> And that Thou bidst me come to Thee,
> O Lamb of God, I come.

What a new light these circumstances shed on such words as those of the third verse:

> Just as I am, though tossed about
> With many a conflict, many a doubt,
> Fightings within and fears without,
> O Lamb of God, I come.

After a while her sister-in-law came in to tell her of the progress of the bazaar; and, after reading the hymn, asked—as well she might!—for a copy. So it stole out from that quiet room of suffering to bring its message to thousands and to be of untold blessing to the world! No wonder that the Rev. H. V. Elliott wrote, in after-years : " In the course of a long ministry I hope I have been permitted to see some fruit of my labours; but I feel far more has been done by this single hymn of my sister's."

Chapter 7

## *The Fruit of Pain*

In the next chapter reference is made to the various imaginary stories of the writing by Charles Wesley of the hymn " Jesu, Lover of my soul," stories really based upon the language of the hymn itself. A similar instance of the play of imagination is connected with Dr. George Matheson's delightful verses, beginning " O Love, that wilt not let me go," a hymn which deserves a far wider use than it has at present attained, and to which Dr. A. L. Peace has set a most beautiful tune, adapted to the unusual metre of the lines.

The story has been repeated again and again of the author's marriage engagement, which was followed by the loss of his sight, with the result that his fiancée, on hearing of his blindness, broke off the compact, and that it was after receiving her letter announcing her decision that he sat down and wrote this hymn. Two of its verses would appear to express exactly his feeling under such circumstances:

O Love, that wilt not let me go,
   I rest my weary soul in Thee,
I give Thee back the life I owe,
That in Thine ocean depths its flow
   May richer, fuller be.

O Joy that seekest me through pain,
  I cannot close my heart to Thee,
I trace the rainbow through the rain,
And feel the promise is not vain,
  That morn shall tearless be.

But here again the story is purely imaginary, inspired, no doubt, by the phraseology of the hymn, and by the knowledge that Dr. Matheson had lost his sight.

The writer has been recently assured by Dr. Matheson's sister that the story of these circumstances is entirely unfounded. As a matter of fact, Dr. Matheson became blind in his youth, while the hymn was not written until 1882, when he was forty years of age.

At that time, Miss Matheson says, he had sustained a sad bereavement, and that it was whilst alone and brooding over his sorrow that the words were suddenly suggested to him, and were, to use his own expression, " the inspiration of a moment ".

The lines were written on a summer evening, in the Manse at Innellan, Argyllshire, the parish of which Dr. Matheson was minister. The author himself said of his hymn : " It was composed with extreme rapidity; it seemed to me that its construction only occupied a few minutes, and I felt myself rather in the position of one who was being dictated to than of an original artist. I was suffering from extreme mental distress, and the hymn was the fruit of pain."

119

# In the School Playground

One December day in 1871, Frances Ridley Havergal, then visiting a friend, Mr. Snepp of Perry Barr (who next year edited *Songs of Grace and Glory*) walked with him to the boys' school, and, while he went in, leaned against the playground wall to rest, as she was very tired.

When Mr. Snepp returned ten minutes later he found Miss Havergal busily scribbling on an old envelope. At his request she gave him the hymn which she had just written, and which has become very popular in America, though not so well-known in this country.

The first verse, composed amid such apparently inappropriate surroundings, runs thus:

> Golden harps are sounding,
>   Angel voices sing,
> Pearly gates are opened,
>   Opened for the King;
> Jesus, King of Glory,
>   Jesus, King of Love,
> Is gone up in triumph
>   To His throne above.
>
> All His work is ended,
>   Joyfully we sing;
> Jesus hath ascended!
>   Glory to our King!

For this hymn Miss Havergal afterwards composed her stirring tune " Hermas," the tune which was on her lips when, eight years later, on June 3, 1879, the " pearly gates " opened for her, and she passed into the Presence of her King.

## During the Epidemic

In the month of July, 1864, an epidemic was raging in the city of Brooklyn, which was then the home of Dr. Robert Lowry. One hot afternoon Dr. Lowry was seated in his study, his thought occupied with the reason for hymn-writers saying so much about the river of death and so little about the river of the water of life which St. John saw flowing through the streets of the new Jerusalem.

As he sat wrapt in thought, there suddenly came to him the words of a new hymn. These he hurriedly wrote down, and then, turning to the organ which stood in his room, he straightway composed the tune which probably is sung to his words in the great majority of the world's Sunday Schools. So came into being the hymn :

> Shall we gather at the river,
>   Where bright angel feet have trod,
> With its crystal tide for ever
>   Flowing by the throne of God?

Dr. Lowry himself did not think very highly of his own musical composition, which he said owed its popularity to its lilt and swing rather than to its excellence.

It does not seem to have occurred to him to notice the inaccuracy of the last line of the above verse, which is repeated in the chorus.

The river, as described in Revelation 22 : 1, to which the hymn refers, does not flow " by " the throne of God, but " out of " it, a very different thing. It is really a symbolical description of the Holy Spirit " proceeding from the Father and the Son ". But it is a common fault of hymn-writers to treat the symbolical language of Scripture as if it were literal.

## Completed in Thirty Minutes

In the village of Elkhorn, in Wisconsin, U.S.A. lived a musician and composer, Mr. J. P. Webster. Of an extremely sensitive nature, he was frequently attacked by fits of melancholy and depression. One of his friends, Mr. S. F. Bennett, who resided in the same village, found that these moods could often be dispelled by giving the musician a new hymn or song which needed music written for it.

On one such occasion Mr. Bennett was sitting writing in his office, when Webster entered and walked to the fire, turning his back upon his friend without a word.

Bennett asked him what was the matter, and only received a curt and indefinite reply to the effect that " it would be all right by and by."

Instantly the last three words of Webster's answer flashed the idea of a hymn into Bennett's mind.

" The sweet by and by!" he said; " would not that make a good hymn?"

Webster answered in an uninterested tone that " it might," but Bennett, turning to his desk, wrote down, as fast as his pen could cover the paper, the first three verses and chorus of the world-famous hymn, best known by that title. When finished he handed the manuscript to Webster. The musician's interest was awakened, his whole aspect changed; turning to the desk, he began, equally rapidly, to compose a melody for the stirring words. He then requested one of two other friends, who had come in, to lend him his violin, on which he played over the new melody.

Once more he turned to the desk, and wrote down the harmonies for the four parts of the chorus. Within thirty minutes from the time Mr. Bennett wrote the first line the four friends were singing the hymn as it was afterwards published.

During the singing a fifth friend entered, and, after listening, exclaimed with tears in his eyes, " That hymn is immortal!"

A true prophecy, for the world will never forget the touching lines and music thus rapidly put together in the little American village over fifty years ago:

> There's a land that is fairer than day,
>   And by faith we can see it afar,
> For the Father waits, over the way,
>   To prepare us a dwelling-place there.
>
>   In the sweet by and by,
>   We shall meet on that beautiful shore

## The Undergraduate and the School Girl

Rather more than a century ago a brilliant undergraduate of Cambridge University was sitting for his mathematical examination. Having finished all the problems which had been set, and having to remain in the examination room for the full period of time allowed, he occupied himself by writing on the back of his examination paper the first ten lines of the hymn now known by its opening words:

Oft in danger, oft in woe,

although these particular words were really an emenddation of later times.

Some sixteen years afterwards the paper, with Kirke White's lines still on the back, came into the possession of Mrs. Fuller-Maitland, who was compiling a hymn book.

She could not, of course, use an unfinished hymn but she showed the paper to her daughter Frances, a schoolgirl of fourteen, remarking on the pity of its not being complete. The girl took the paper to her own room, and presently brought it back to her mother, with fourteen new lines added, thus making a perfect hymn.

Mrs. Fuller-Maitland published the hymn in her book, and it has now come into almost universal use.

Kirke White entitled his hymn "The Christian Soldier Encouraged," but Frances Fuller-Maitland attained this aim much more successfully than did the original author. The first verse, as the undergraduate wrote it, is decidedly depressing:

Much in sorrow, oft in woe,
Onward, Christians, onward go,
Fight the fight, and, worn with strife,
Steep with tears the bread of life.

124

It was the schoolgirl who wrote the stirring lines:

> Let your drooping hearts be glad;
> March in heavenly armour clad;
> Fight, nor think the battle long,
> Victory soon shall tune your song.

## From Theory to Practice

Both the words and music of the widely used hymn, "Yield not to temptation," are the work of Mr. H. R. Palmer. The author says that the hymn was an inspiration which came to him while he was studying the dry subject of "Theory"; the whole idea of both words and music came to him instantaneously, and putting aside his theoretical work, he wrote them both down as fast as his pen could move.

On the suggestion of a friend some slight changes were made in the third verse, and the tune was afterwards transposed from the key of A flat to that of B flat, otherwise the composition is exactly as it came that day from Mr. Palmer's pen.

## The Steps of the Staircase

In the year 1872 two ladies were conversing together on the subject, dear to both their hearts, of the Return of Our Lord, and one of them quoted a line from the writings of Anna Shipton, "This may be the day of His Coming", adding her testimony to the joy and comfort she found in the thought.

Mr. P. P. Bliss, the well-known hymn-writer, was sitting near, and overheard the conversation which impressed him more deeply than ever before with the reality of the Second Advent.

A few days later the same thought was occupying his mind as he was slowly descending the stairs from his room, when he commenced singing, on the spur of the moment, the lines of his widely known hymn :

Down life's dark vale we wander
  Till Jesus comes;
We watch, and wait, and wonder,
  Till Jesus comes.
Oh, let my lamp be burning,
  When Jesus comes;
For Him my soul be yearning,
  When Jesus comes.

As Mr. Bliss took step after step down the staircase, so the words and music together were given him—indeed, one can almost hear the singer stepping slowly down the stairs as one repeats the lines.

He then wrote the hymn and music down, just as it appeared in the first collection of hymns published by Moody and Sankey.

## The Medical Missions

Somewhere about 1898 I had a long train journey from London to the north of England. Alone in the carriage, towards the end of the journey, the thought occurred to me that a good hymn for Medical Missions abroad could be founded on the incident so well described to the opening verse of Canon Twells' beautiful hymn, " At even, ere the sun was set."

Taking pencil and paper, I proceeded to set down verses to succeed that well-known first verse, but on this different subject. Being afterwards submitted to competent judges, this new version was warmly approved, and Canon Twells having most generously and kindly allowed the use of his opening lines, the hymn was published in the *Church Missionary Hymn Book,* set to the usual tune " Angelus," and has been somewhat widely used.

It may be of interest to the readers of these pages if I venture to quote some of the verses, beginning with the second, which follows that of Canon Twells:

Fast falls the world's great eventide,
  Her sun is sinking in the sky;
And still, O Lord, on every side
  Her sick and suffering round Thee lie.

'Mid heathen ignorance and gloom,
  By untold maladies oppressed,
They sink in anguish to the tomb,
  Unhealed, uncomforted, unblest.

O Saviour, Thou art with us still,
  Through other hands Thy touch we feel,
Thou workest yet by human skill,
  Thy power is present still to heal.

The last verse ends with the repetition of the original hymn's beautiful closing line:

Stretch forth, O Lord, Thy hand of power,
  As o'er the world the shadows fall,
Hear, in this last and solemn hour,
  And in Thy mercy heal us all.

## *All but Burnt*

On January 10, 1858, Miss Frances Ridley Havergal, then staying with a German minister, came in tired and weary, and sat down in her host's study. On the wall opposite hung a picture of our Blessed Lord on the Cross, and underneath were the words " I did this for thee; what hast thou done for Me?"

As Miss Havergal sat there, the Saviour's eyes seemed to rest upon her, and, on reading the words below the picture, her now well-known and beautiful hymn seemed to flash into her mind:

> I gave My life for thee,
>   My precious Blood I shed,
> That thou might'st ransomed be,
>   And quickened from the dead.
> I gave My life for thee;
> What hast thou given for Me?

Snatching up a piece of paper, Miss Havergal hurriedly scribbled down the above and following verses of the hymn, but, appealing as the words have been to many, they did not then appear so to her. On the contrary, she thought them so poor and unsatisfactory that she decided not to trouble to write them out properly, and tossed the paper on to the fire. Happily it fell from the grate to the hearth, undestroyed although crumpled and singed, whereupon the author changed her mind and put the verses aside.

Soon after, happening to visit an old woman in an almshouse, she thought she would see whether these verses would appeal to the simple old woman, feeling sure that no one else would be likely to care for them.

But the old lady was so delighted with them that Miss Havergal then copied them out afresh and eventually showed them to her father, the Rev. William Havergal, who not only persuaded her to keep them, but also wrote for them the tune " Baca ", to which they are so often sung. A year later they were published in leaflet form, and the next year appeared in *Good Words*.

In several hymn-books the hymn has been recast, so as to be addressed by us to Christ instead of by Christ to us, probably being considered as more suitable for public worship in that form. So in this revision the first line reads :

Thy life was given for Me.

Miss Havergal made no objection to this alteration, inasmuch as the sentiment of the hymn remained unchanged, but she preferred her own original version as being the most appealing and effective, with which many will agree.

## *The Appeal of the Third Verse*

When Prebendary W. St. Hill Bourne wrote his beautiful and widely used harvest hymn, " The Sower went forth sowing," he was a young clergyman, in charge of a church at South Ashford, Kent, with a congregation largely consisting of railway men and their families.

On the proprietors of *Hymns Ancient and Modern* obtaining permission to use this hymn in one of their new editions, and no special tune having been written for it, they sent it to Sir Frederick Bridge at Westminster Abbey, asking him to compose a suitable tune.

Sir Frederick received this request just at the time when his little daughter Beatrice lay dying, and it can be well understood how, under such circumstances, the words of the third verse would appeal to the father's heart:

> Within a hallowed acre
> He sows yet other grain,
> Where peaceful earth receiveth
> The dead He died to gain;
> For, though the growth be hidden,
> We know that they shall rise;
> Yea, even now they ripen
> In sunny Paradise.
>
> O summer land of harvest!
> O fields for ever white
> With souls that wear Christ's raiment,
> With crowns of golden light.

Such was the effect of these lovely lines that Sir Frederick himself declared the writing of his tune for them to be different from any other work which he had ever done. To that fact is due, no doubt, the exquisite beauty of the music, which, in memory of the beloved little daughter, the composer named " St. Beatrice."

## During the Haymaking

Few hymns for an after-meeting are more effective than that written by the Rev. W. E. Witter, with its tender and touching appeal:

While Jesus whispers to you,
    Come, sinner, come!
While we are praying for you,
    Come, sinner, come!
Now is the time to own Him,
    Come, sinner, come!
Now is the time to know Him,
    Come, sinner, come!

The author says that the hymn was written in the summer of 1877, when he was a student at college, but had returned home on account of his mother's serious illness. He had been reading the biography of Mr. P. P. Bliss, and the words of his sacred songs were constantly in Mr. Witter's mind, leading him to pray that he too might be inspired to write some hymn that would reach the hearts of men and help to lead them to Christ.

It was on a Saturday afternoon that the answer to the prayer was given. Along the roadside the grass had been cut for hay, and Mr. Witter was helping to fork it up into haycocks, when the words of this hymn seemed to sing themselves into his heart, to a melody very like the music afterwards composed for them by Mr. H. R. Palmer.

Leaving the haymaking, he hurried to the house, and, kneeling beside the bed in his brother's room, began to write down on paper the words that were still in his mind. He did this, he says " with a strange consciousness that they were God-given, and that God would use them ". It goes without saying that this feeling has been abundantly justified by the blessing brought through Mr. Witter's lines to many souls.

## In the Stage-Coach

In the year 1841 a young lady, aged twenty-eight, by name Miss Jemima Thompson, began to attend the Normal Infant School in Gray's Inn Road, London, in order to obtain some knowledge of the system ot teaching.

Among the pieces played when the children were marching was a Greek air, which pleased Miss Thompson very much, and which she felt would form an admirable tune for a children's hymn if she could only find words to fit it. But the rhythm of the music was very unusual and although Miss Thompson searched through various Sunday School and other hymn-books, she failed to find anything that would suit the measure of the melody.

After a time she was obliged to return to her home, and soon after travelled on some missionary business to the little town of Wellington, journeying in a stage-coach. It was an hour's ride, and a beautiful spring morning, and except herself there was no other inside passenger. Then there came to her mind once more the haunting strains of the marching tune, and taking an old envelope from her pocket she wrote, in pencil, the first two verses of one of the most delightful children's hymns ever composed, intending them simply for the use of the children in the village school, but which—with an additional verse added later in order to give the hymn a missionary character—have become famous the world over, the first of them being,

I think when I read that sweet story of old,
  When Jesus was here among men,
How He called little children as lambs to His fold,
  I should like to have been with him then.
I wish that His hands had been placed on my head,
  That His arms had been thrown around me,
And that I might have seen His kind look when He said,
  " Let the little ones come unto Me."

Mr. Thompson, the authoress's father, was superintendent of the Sunday School in the village, and his custom was to let the children choose the first hymn each Sunday. One Sunday they started " I think when I read that sweet story of old," which they had learned in the day school. Mr. Thompson turned to his younger daughters and said :

" Where did that come from? I never heard it before."

To which they replied, " Oh, Jemima made it."

The next day he asked for a copy, and sent it, without Miss Thompson's knowledge, to *The Sunday School Teacher's Magazine,* except for which action it would probably never have appeared in print.

It will be observed that the hymn was originally written in three verses of eight lines each, though each verse is now usually divided into two verses of four lines. It is remarkable indeed that the writer of such a beautiful sacred lyric, who began her contributions to *The Juvenile Magazine* at the age of thirteen, and afterwards published several works, yet never composed another hymn.

She herself says, however, regarding her hymn : " It was a little inspiration from above, and not ' in

me,' for I have never written other verses worthy of
preservation."


## The First English Hymn Writer

It may be of interest to my readers to know that
the first hymn written in English, or rather in the
Anglo-Saxon language of that age, was composed by
a man named Cædmon towards the close of the seventh
century.

The story of its origin is remarkable, for Cædmon
until quite late in life was so ignorant of singing or
music that when, at some entertainment, it was
arranged that every one should sing in turn, a harp
being passed from one to another, he, when his turn
was approaching, would leave the feast and return
home.

On one such occasion, instead of going to his own
house, he went to the stable, which had been placed
under his charge for the night, and lay down to sleep.

During the night he had a dream of some one
standing by him and calling him by his name, saying:

"Cædmon, sing me something", to which he
replied:

"I know not how to sing; and for that reason
I went out from the entertainment and retired hither,
because I could not sing."

"Yet you have something to sing to me", replied
the one who had called him.

"What must I sing", enquired Cædmon, to which
the reply was:

" Sing the beginning of created things "; whereupon he, who had never sung in his life before, began to sing entirely original verse in praise of God the Creator.

On rising from sleep he found that he could remember all that he had sung in his dream, and from that time he continued to compose many such beautiful verses and hymns by the power thus remarkably given to him by God.

# Chapter 8

POINTS OF INTEREST IN THE

LANGUAGE OF HYMNS

## *A Popular Fallacy*

In almost every hymn-book Lyte's famous hymn, " Abide with me," is placed with the Evening Hymns, the only exceptions known to the writer being *The English Hymnal* and *Church Hymns.* Yet the idea that " Abide with me " is an evening hymn is entirely fallacious, and arises from a misunderstanding of the author's meaning.

It is possible that the similarity of the opening words of the hymn to the two lines in Keble's " Sun of my soul."

> Abide with me from morn till eve

and

> Abide with me when night is nigh,

have led to the idea that Lyte's reference also is to the natural day. But this is quite mistaken, since it is obvious that the words of Luke 24: 19: " Abide with us, for it is toward evening, and the day is far spent ", are taken by him in an entirely figurative sense, and that his reference is to the approach of Life's eventide and the closing of Life's day. The third line of the first verse makes this perfectly clear :

> When other helpers fail and comforts flee,

which could not apply to the ordinary approach of evening; while the second verse expresses the writer's idea in unmistakable terms :

> Swift to its close ebbs out *Life's little day.*

As already related, the hymn was written on September 4, 1847, and its author died on November 20 of the same year, showing that it was his sense of the falling of his own life's eventide which inspired the hymn.

## *The Unknown Author*

One of the best loved hymns of the Christian Church is that commencing " Jerusalem, my happy home," which, in the form we know, first appeared in 1795. The Rector of Eckington, in the days when many parishes issued their own collections of hymns, desired Mr. Joseph Bromehead to revise the *Eckington Psalms and Hymns* then in use, the new book containing what would seem to us the extremely meagre number of forty-seven metrical psalms and thirty-seven hymns!

In this book the hymn consisted of seven stanzas, the one almost invariably omitted nowadays being,

O when, thou city of my God,
Shall I thy courts ascend,
Where congregations ne'er break up,
And Sabbaths have no end.

Probably the unpoetical character of the third line has caused the general omission of the verse.

Bromehead, however, did not compose the original hymn. In his preface to the book he says: " I should have liked to prefix the author's name to every psalm or hymn; but of some I did not know the authors, and in others I have used so much liberty of altering and inserting lines and stanzas as to leave the claim of authorship doubtful."

This particular hymn falls under both the above heads. The original " Jerusalem, my happy home," has only for the author's signature the initials " F.B.P." Various guesses have been made as to the person whom these initials represent, but all that one can say is that the hymn was written in the sixteenth or seventeenth century, that its author was probably a Roman Catholic, and that possibly he was a priest.

The original hymn, too, is very different from the amended version as we known it. Instead of seven verses, it had twenty-six, and some of these are so quaint as to be unsuitable for modern use. Nevertheless both the *English Hymnal* and the *Oxford Hymn Book* include one of these, viz.:

Within thy gates no thing doth come
That is not passing clean,
No spider's web, no dirt, no dust,
No filth may there be seen.

One cannot but feel that the compilers of these hymnals must have been a trifle lacking in a saving sense of humour, however attractive this verse might be to housemaids! Both books, moreover, include the following curious verses, which are given here in their original spelling and lack of any punctuation:

> There cinomon there sugar groes
> There narde and blame abound
> What tongue can tell or hart conceue
> The joyes that there are found
>
> There David standes with harpe in hand
> As maister of the Queere
> Tenne thousand times that man were blest
> That might this musicke hear
>
> Our Ladie singes magnificat
> With tune surpassing sweete
> And all the virginns beare their parts
> Sitinge aboue her feete
>
> Te Deum doth Sant Ambrose singe
> Saint Augustine dothe the like
> Ould Simeon and Zacharie
> Haue not their songes to seeke
>
> There Magdalene hath left her mone
> And cheerefullie doth singe
> With blessed Saints whose harmonie
> In everie streete doth ringe.

## The Altered Line

In Toplady's great hymn, "Rock of Ages," there is one line which has been much criticised and frequently amended, namely, the second line of the fourth verse:

When my eye-strings break in death,

a line which is not only harsh, but quite inaccurate. Some of the various emendations, such as:

> When mine eyelids close in death,

or

> When my heart-strings break in death,

or

> When mine eyes are closed in death.

are quite as unsatisfactory; heart-strings do not " break in death," nor do eyes or eyelids " close," but have to *be* closed after death. The best emendation of the line, therefore, is:

> When mine eyes are closed in death.

## The Four Versions

Next to her " Just as I am, without one plea," the most widely used hymns written by Miss Charlotte Elliott is the one beginning, " My God, my Father, while I stray." It is probably the only hymn existing of which the composer published no less than four different versions! It is true that the differences between them are not very great, but it has led to some confusion as to the true text. One of her verses is frequently omitted in modern hymnals, namely:

> Should grief or sickness waste away
> My life in premature decay;
> My father, still I'll strive to say
> Thy Will be done.

## Only Six Words Left

Several of our well-known hymns are from the pen of the Rev. J. H. Gurney, who wrote, " Lord, as to Thy dear Cross we flee "; " Great King of nations, hear our prayer "; and the beautiful child's hymn, " Fair waved the golden corn."

But the most famous of his hymns, and the most widely used, namely, " We saw Thee not when Thou didst come," has a curious history. Gurney himself tells us that it was suggested by a poem in a small American volume, " which was well conceived but very imperfectly executed ".

The form in which the Misses Carus-Wilson first published a similar hymn in England, in 1834, may have been drawn from this poem, though not identical with it; it opens thus :

> We have not seen Thy footsteps tread
> This wild and sinful earth of ours,
> Nor heard Thy Voice restore the dead
> Again to life's reviving powers;
> But we believe—for all things are
> The gifts of Thine Almighty care.

The American poem, however, as we shall see, must have begun differently.

Four years later, Gurney, then Curate of Lutterworth, also published an adaptation of the American poem in a *Collection of Hymns for Public Worship. His* first verse was as follows :

141

> We saw Thee not when Thou didst tread
>   In mortal guise this sinful earth,
> Nor heard Thy voice restore the dead,
>   And wake them to a second birth;
> But we believe that Thou didst come,
> And leave for us Thy glorious home.

Quite obviously these two versions were drawn from the same unknown source.

But in 1851, Gurney, at the time Rector of St. Mary's, Marylebone, republished the hymn in the form we now use. It will be observed that the first verse (as the others) is considerably altered, and now runs :

> We saw Thee not when Thou didst come
>   To this poor world of sin and death,
> Nor e'en beheld Thy cottage home
>   In that despisèd Nazareth;
> But we believe Thy footsteps trod
> Its streets and plains, Thou Son of God.

The fourth verse of this hymn is almost identical with one in the version published by Misses Carus-Wilson. But the original poem is evidently lost, for in his *Marylebone Hymn Book* Mr. Gurney tells us, in a note on this hymn, that " nothing of the original composition remains, but the *first* four words, and the *repeated* words ". All, therefore, that survives from the pen of the original author are the six words :

> " We saw Thee not,"

and

> " We believe."

## The Childless Authoress

It is not a little surprising to know that Mrs. Albert Smith, the writer of the popular hymn, " Let us gather up the sunbeams," better known by its chorus title, " Scatter seeds of kindness," had no children. Yet her love for children must have been very great, for no mother could have written more tender and beautiful lines than hers, with reference to the little ones whom God has called back to Himself :

> Ah ! those little ice-cold fingers,
>   How they point our memories back
> To the hasty words and actions
>   Strewn along our backward track!
> How those little hands remind us,
>   As in snowy grace they lie,
> Not to scatter thorns, but roses
>   For our reaping by-and-by.

## Fiction and Fact

There is probably no hymn concerning the origin of which so many varied stories have been told as Charles Wesley's famous " Jesu, Lover of my soul ". One version ascribes the idea of the hymn to a bird flying from a hawk and taking refuge in Wesley's bosom as he sat at an open window; another to a sea-bird doing the same during a great storm at sea; a third to Wesley's own deliverance from the peril of a hurricane encountered when he was on a voyage; a fourth to his hiding under a hedge in Ireland from a band of enemies, writing the hymn while his pursuers searched for him in vain.

The first of these stories is very attractive, and is probably the most frequently repeated, but truthfulness compels one to say frankly that there is not the least foundation for the historical accuracy of any of them; they have almost certainly been suggested by the hymn itself instead of the hymn arising from them!

All that can be said with certainty is that the hymn was written very soon after the great spiritual change which the author experienced in 1738 and within a few months of the date given as that of the founding of Methodism in 1739.

The chief interest of the hymn's history lies in the strong criticism directed to two phrases in the first verse: the description of our Lord as " Lover of my soul," and the line " While the nearer waters roll ".

With regard to the first, the word "Lover" has been objected to as a title which was undignified when applied to the Divine Being, and various substitutes have been printed, such as:

Jesu, Refuge of my soul,

or

Jesu, Saviour of my soul,

or

Father, Refuge of my soul.

None of these are anything like so tender and beautiful as Wesley's original line, and it is difficult to see any objection to it, since St. Paul's words " The Son of

God Who loved me and gave Himself up for me" (Gal. 2 : 20, R.V.), are surely sufficient warrant for the expression, while the actual phrase occurs in the Apocrypha: " Thou sparest all; for they are Thine, O Lord, Thou Lover of souls " (Wisdom of Solomon 11 : 26). Most modern hymn-books have rightly, therefore, retained Wesley's phrase.

More reasonable, perhaps, was the other criticism of his description of the rolling of " the nearest waters "; it was argued that if the waters rolled at all they would all do so, and not just the waves in the immediate neighbourhood, and so we have another series of substituted lines:

or
> While the billows near me roll,

or
> While the raging billows roll,

or
> While the threatening waters roll,

> While the waves around me roll, etc.

Nevertheless, Wesley knew better than his critics. For it is quite within a sailor's experience that a sudden squall may strike a vessel, and lash the waters around it into fury, while in the far distance there is comparative calm; and it is still truer in spiritual experience for a soul to be tempest-tossed by inward passions and temptations, while another knows only calm and peace.

So the first verse of Wesley's beautiful hymn is still sung by most people as he wrote it, although in all more than twenty different changes have been made in the first four lines at various times!

## A Much Altered Hymn

In a reading book published for use in the Boston Primary Schools, U.S.A., in 1845, appeared for the first time the beautiful children's hymn, beginning,

> Little drops of water,
> Little grains of sand,
> Make the mighty ocean
> And the beauteous land.

The authoress of this delightful hymn, which consisted of five verses, was Mrs. Julia A. Carney, a teacher in one of the Boston schools, which, oddly enough, was held in the vestry of Hollis Street Church, in that city!

Three years later a Dr. Brewer calmly appropriated the first verse of Mrs. Carney's hymn, added four other verses of no merit or interest whatever, and published the whole in another school reading book. Here are the commonplace verses which Dr. Brewer substituted for Mrs. Carney's beautiful lines:

> Straw by straw the sparrow
> Builds its cosy nest;
> Leaf by leaf the forest
> Stands in verdure drest.

> Drop by drop is iron
> > Worn in time away;
> Perseverance, patience,
> > Ever win their way.

> Letter after letter
> > Words and books are made;
> Little and by little
> > Mountains level laid.

> Every finished labour
> > Once did but begin;
> Try, and go on trying,
> > That's the way to win.

Mrs. Carney's original hymn, however, was republished, fortunately, in the *American Juvenile Magazine*, whence it was copied into a book of Hymns and Songs, published in Manchester in 1855, and so became known to English children.

Twenty-one years later Bishop Bickersteth made the hymn still more beautiful and complete by adding this verse:

> Little ones in glory,
> > Swell the angel's song,
> Make us meet, dear Saviour,
> > For their holy throng.

Still later, Prebendary Thring expanded this last verse into three stanzas.

## Before or after Sunset?

Few hymns are more widely known or more loved than Canon H. Twells':

> At even, ere the sun was set,
> The sick, O Lord, around Thee lay;

It has been included in almost every known hymn book both in England and in the United States. A most interesting criticism has, however, been directed against its very first line.

Three of the Gospels record the incident enshrined in the opening verse of the hymn, the passages being Matthew 8: 16; Mark 1: 32–34; and Luke 4: 40.

The Jews, of course, reckoned each day from sunset to sunset, and it is clear from St. Mark's account (verse 21) that the day closed by that particular sunset was the Sabbath. But on the Sabbath no Jew would dream of performing any such work as carrying the sick from one place to another, and therefore it is urged that Canon Twells was in error in writing:

At even, *ere* the sun was set,

as it would still be the Sabbath day.

The records of the three evangelists are not perfectly conclusive, as, though St. Matthew says: " When even was come ", and St. Mark: " At even, when the sun did set "—which appear to justify their criticism—St. Luke says: " When the sun was setting ", a phrase which would seem to support Canon Twells' words.

Three emendations, therefore, have been made of the disputed phrase, namely:

At even, ere the sun *did* set,
At even, *when* the sun was set,
At even, *when* the sun did set.

148

Is it possible that the sunset was reckoned to begin as the rim of the sun first touched the horizon? If so, this would solve the difficulty. But in any case, it would seem that the third of the above changes is the best, as simply repeating the very words of Scripture.

A very beautiful verse in the hymn, the fourth, has been widely omitted, probably on account of the length of the hymn, but in one or two more recent hymnals it has been deservedly reinstated. It runs thus :

> And some are pressed with worldly care,
> And some are tried with sinful doubt;
> And some such grievous passions tear,
> That only Thou canst cast them out.

## The Abiding Influence of the Prayer Meeting

It is now over 150 years ago since the Rev. John Newton and his people at Olney gathered week by week in their prayer meeting on Tuesday evenings, but the influence of that meeting has permeated the whole Christian Church, and will never cease to exert its power for good. For to his custom of writing a new hymn every week for this parochial gathering, the Church of God owes some of her most glorious lyrics.

For this meeting were written, and there were sung for the first time, such world-wide favourites as " Hark, my soul, it is the Lord "; " Come, my soul, thy suit prepare "; " There is a fountain filled with blood "; " Approach, my soul, the Mercy-seat "; " Glorious things of thee are spoken" (deemed by many to be Newton's finest hymn, and one of the best in the English language); "How sweet the Name of Jesus sounds".

This latter hymn has always presented one great difficulty, viz.: the titles of our Lord as given in the first line of the fifth verse:

Jesus, my Shepherd, Husband, Friend.

It is argued, and not without reason, that in this form the line is unsuited for use by a general congregation, as our Lord cannot be said to be the "Husband" of *men*. In different hymnals, therefore, there appear various attempts to overcome this difficulty, and we have the following modifications of the line:

Jesus, our Leader, Shepherd, Friend;

Jesus, my Shepherd, Surety, Friend;

Jesus, our Shepherd, Brother, Friend;

Jesus, my Shepherd, Guardian, Friend;

Jesus, my Saviour, Shepherd, Friend!

although some books still retain the original line.

How marvellous it is that from this weekly gathering, in the obscure little town of Olney, should have gone forth a stream of sacred melody that has enriched the whole world for all time. What an illustration of the truth of the old words "A little one shall become a thousand . . . I the Lord will hasten it in his time" (Isa. 60: 22).

## The Mystery of the Last Lines

Beautiful as are the closing lines of Newman's great hymn, "Lead, kindly Light," there has been a great variety of opinion as to what he really meant when he wrote:

> And with the morn those angel faces smile,
> Which I have loved long since, and lost awhile.

Some have believed them to refer to the "angel faces" of Faith, Hope, and Assurance, which, shining bright in the earlier years of spiritual experience, in later years became dim and distant.

Others see here a reference to those angels whom God sends forth to minister to the heirs of salvation.

Others, again, consider that the lines refer to the reunion of the Christian with those dear to him on earth who have previously passed away; while, yet again, others read into the words the description of the awakening of the soul at the end of life, when the business and cares and pleasures of this world are losing their hold, and the beauties of the other life begin to dawn. Which of these is the true view?

Newman himself was asked this question in the year 1880, and his reply should, of course, be conclusive. But all he said was that at the end of the fifty years since the lines were written he could not himself remember what he really meant! So we shall never know!

Chapter 9

## The Lay of the Last Minstrel

One of the greatest and grandest of the old Latin hymns is that known as *Dies Irae,* of which it has been said " every word is weighty, yea, even a thunder-clap ". It was probably the composition of a Franciscan Friar named Thomas of Celano, who lived in the thirteenth century. English people, of course, know it best in its translated forms, two being especially familiar.

The original hymn consisted of twenty-two verses of three lines each, but one of the most widely used English forms is that condensed into only three verses of four lines, beginning, " That day of wrath, that dreadful day." But few who use the hymn know that its author was Sir Walter Scott, and that the three verses are taken from his most famous poem, " The Lay of the Last Minstrel." In that work the poet is describing the monks of Melrose Abbey and their service in the days of old :

With snow-white stoles in order due
The holy fathers two and two
    In long procession came;
And far the echoing aisles prolong
The awful burden of their song;

That day of wrath, that dreadful day,
When heaven and earth shall pass away,
What power shall be the sinner's stay?
How shall he meet that dreadful day?

## The Archbishop's Funeral Sermon

The fullest and best translation of *Dies Irae*, however, is that by Dr. W. J. Irons, which was inspired by unusual circumstances. During the French Revolution in 1848 the Archbishop of Paris was shot dead on one of the barricades in the city, while he was endeavouring to persuade the insurgents to cease firing, and was buried on July 7 of that year.

It was not considered safe at the moment to have a funeral sermon in his memory, but as soon as possible this took place in the cathedral of Notre Dame, accompanied by a most impressive and solemn service, throughout which the deceased Archbishop's heart was exposed in a glass case in the choir of the cathedral, while at the appointed place the *Dies Irae* was sung, of course in Latin, by an immense body of priests.

The wonderful rendering of this great hymn by the massed voices, together with the peculiarly solemn surroundings, the exposed heart of the Archbishop, the deep sense of bereavement, and the terror of the times, made the service most remarkably impressive, and Dr. Irons, who was present, was deeply moved both by the singing and the whole scene.

As soon as the service was over he went home

and wrote his translation of the great hymn, a translation by far the finest of the 133 renderings into
English of the great Latin original, and one which
doubtless owes much of its power and beauty to the
impression produced by the scene in the cathedral. As
Dr. Irons wrote it, the first verse ran,

> Day of wrath, O day of mourning,
> See once more the Cross returning—[1]
> Heaven and earth in ashes burning.

The translator's last two lines ran,

> Lord, Who didst our souls redeem,
> Grant a blessèd Requiem!

for which, in most hymn-books, are substituted the
lines of another translator;

> Lord all-pitying, Jesu blest,
> Grant them Thine eternal rest.

It is remarkable that when Sir Walter Scott was
on his death-bed he was heard repeating over and
over one verse, from the longer Latin version, which
in Dr. Iron's translation runs,

> Faint and weary Thou has sought me,
> On the Cross of suffering brought me;
> Shall such grace in vain be brought me?

---

[1] The second line has reference to the formerly widespread
belief, founded on Matt. 24: 30, that at the approach of the
Second Advent the Cross would appear in the sky.

## The Two Tunes

Dr. Rankin, the author of the hymn whose popularity is world-wide, namely, " God be with you till we meet again," says that it was written in 1882 simply as a Christian " good-bye," that it was not called forth by any person or any special occasion, but was simply composed on the basis of the etymological meaning of the word " good-bye," which is " God be with you."

That the hymn owes much of its usefulness to Mr. Tomer's tune, to which it is always sung, is unquestioned, and it is therefore of great interest to know that, when the hymn was written, Dr. Rankin sent a copy of the first verse to two different composers, one well known, and the other unknown and not even a competent musician, with the request that they would submit a tune for the hymn.

When these arrived, and Dr. Rankin had examined them, he selected the tune from the unknown composer, showed it to the organist of his church, who suggested one or two amendments, had it sung at one of his services, and adopted the tune for his hymn, in conjunction with which it has proved of immense value. Mr. Tomer was a school teacher when he wrote the tune at Dr. Rankin's request.

## In the State Prison

A remarkable incident, illustrating the power of Mr. Palmer's hymn, " Yield not to temptation," took place in the State Prison at Sing Sing, New York. At that time women were confined there as well as men, and on one occasion, when the women were allowed to sit in the corridor to listen to an address from a lady, the prisoners rebelled against an order given by the matron, resulting in a terrible scene, during which screams, ribaldry, blasphemy and profanity filled the place. The matron had sent for help, when suddenly a voice rose above the tumult, singing,

> Yield not to temptation,
> For yielding is sin.

It was one of the prisoners' favourite hymns, and as the words pealed out, first quiet began to prevail, then the women joined in the hymn, and finally marched quietly back to their cells.

## The Child's Additional Verse

A good many years ago a lady was returning from an evangelistic meeting, accompanied by her little daughter, only eight years of age. At the meeting the hymn beginning "Knocking, knocking, who is there?" had been sung, and on the way home the child referred to the last verse, which ends,

> Yes, the piercèd Hand still knocketh,
> And beneath the crownèd hair
> Beam the patient eyes, so tender,
> Of thy Saviour, waiting there.

"Mother," said the little girl, "I don't think the hymn ought to end like that, because, you see, it leaves the Saviour still standing outside!"

The mother thought no more of her child's remark, but on reaching home her little daughter disappeared for a time, remaining in her own room. When at length she came downstairs again, she gave her mother a piece of paper, saying:

" There, mother, I think it ought to have something at the end like that."

The mother, greatly astonished, unfolded the paper, and read the verse her little child had written :

Enter! enter! Heavenly Guest!
Welcome! welcome to my breast!
I have long withstood Thy knocking,
    For my heart was full of sin;
But Thy love hath overcome me,
    Blessèd Jesus!—O come in!

The mother, as well she might be, was so impressed with her little daughter's additional verse that she sent it to a religious paper, explaining the circumstances of its composition. There it caught the eye of the Rev. Canon Hay Aitken, who was so struck by it that he added it to the original hymn in the *Church Parochial Mission Hymn Book*.

## Saved from the Fire

On February 9, 1709, at Epworth Rectory, the Rector, the Rev. Samuel Wesley, sat in his room writing the following lines :

Behold the Saviour of mankind
    Nailed to the shameful tree!
How vast the love that Him inclined
    To bleed and die for thee!

157

It was the beginning of a new hymn for Good Friday. Having completed its four verses, the Rector left the manuscript near the window, and presently retired to rest.

That night the Rectory caught fire, and the whole building, with all its contents, was utterly destroyed. In one room slept little John Wesley, aged five, with his three sisters, the baby and the nurse. On the alarm being given, the nurse seized the baby and rushed from the room, calling to the other children to follow her, which they did, with the exception of John, who was still fast asleep.

Waking soon after, he found his escape cut off by the flames, but climbed the chest which stood by the window, where he was quickly observed. His father made two attempts to reach him by the stairs, but was beaten back by the flames. There was no time to fetch a ladder, but a spectator urged a smaller man to climb on his shoulders and try to reach the child at the window, which he succeeded in doing at the second attempt.

Hardly had he lifted the boy out to safety than the whole roof fell in, fortunately falling inward, or the child and his rescuers would have been killed.

" Come neighbours," cried the Rector, as he clasped John in his arms, " let us kneel down; let us give thanks to God! He has given me all my eight children; let the house go; I am rich enough!"

Yet that night there was one other escape from the flames. Later on, someone walking in the Rectory garden, near the ruins of the house, noticed a piece of paper lying on the ground, and picked it up. It was the Rector's new hymn, blown through the open window from the burning house, which, like John Wesley himself, was thus saved from the fire!

## The Prophetic Lines

The author of the well-known hymn " Come, Thou Fount of every blessing," was a Norfolk lad named Robert Robinson. His was a chequered career. His widowed mother's ambition was to see her son a clergyman of the Church of England, but poverty forbidding the fulfilment of her ambition, the boy was apprenticed to a barber and hairdresser in London at the age of fourteen. He was a bookish lad, and his occupation was anything but congenial.

In the seventeenth year, in company with some of his companions, he joined in making an old fortune-teller intoxicated, in order to make fun of her predictions concerning them. One of her predictions about Robinson was that he should see his children and grandchildren, which, instead of amusing him, turned him to serious thought.

This was quickly followed by the hearing of a solemn sermon from George Whitefield on " The wrath to come " (Matt. 3: 7), from which day, Sunday, May 24, 1752, Robinson dated his new life in Christ.

Six years later he wrote his famous hymn above mentioned. But, in the light of his subsequent history, some of its lines seem tragically prophetic:

Prone to wander, Lord, I feel it;
Prone to leave the God I love.

It is said that, towards the end of his life, when again he had given way to frivolous habits, he was once travelling by stage-coach with a lady, an entire stranger, who in the course of conversation spoke of Robinson's hymn and the blessing it had brought to her soul.

The author vainly attempted to turn the conversation into other channels, but when the lady persisted in referring to his hymn, he became agitated beyond control, and exclaimed:

"Madam, I am the poor, unhappy man who composed that hymn many years ago; and I would give a thousand worlds, if I had them, to enjoy the feelings I had then!"

## From the Prison Window

The legend of the origin of the Latin hymn *Gloria laus et honor* (familiar to us in the English translation beginning "All glory laud and honour") is interesting, although the historical accuracy cannot be entirely vouched for.

St. Theodulph of Orleans, about the year 820, was imprisoned by King Louis the Pious in the cloister at Angers. On Palm Sunday, 821, the King, who was at Angers, took part in the usual procession of clergy and laity, and as they passed St. Theodulph's prison, the saint, standing at the window of his cell, sang this hymn, which he had just composed, all the people standing in silence to listen.

The King was so delighted with the hymn that he set St. Theodulph at liberty, restored him to his see, and ordered that henceforth the hymn should always be used in procession on Palm Sunday.

" The story is not, however, a contemporary one; and moreover it seems clear that Louis the Pious was never in Angers after 818. It is also almost certain that St. Theodulph was never really restored to his see, but that he died at Angers in 821." (James Mearns, M.A., in Julian's *Dictionary of Hymnology,* revised 1907.)

The hymn is founded on Ps. 26: 7-10; Ps. 118: 25, 26; Matt. 21: 1-16 and Luke 19: 37, 38.

In its original form it consisted of no less than thirty-nine verses in our English translation. In translations in common use the first line begins,

All glory, laud, and honour.
Glory, and laud, and honour.
Glory, laud, and honour be, Our Redeemer Christ to Thee.
To Thee be glory, honour, praise.
Glory and praise to Thee, Redeemer blest.
King and Redeemer! To Thee be the glory.
Glory and honour, and laud be to Thee, King Christ the Redeemer.

## The Translation on the Death-bed

The Rev. Thomas Whytehead, at the age of twenty-six, was appointed chaplain to Dr. Selwyn, the Bishop-elect of New Zealand. He sailed for that colony in

1842, but he never did any work in his new sphere, as he ruptured a blood-vessel soon after landing and died after a few months' illness.

During his last days he occupied what little strength he had in correcting the translations of the Bible and Prayer Book into the Maori language, while just before his death he also translated into that tongue Ken's Evening Hymn, " Glory to Thee, my God, this night," the metre and the rhythm being identical with the English, the first instance of a translation of that kind. Two hundred and fifty copies of the new hymn were printed, and were sung by the natives in church and school, while some of them came and sang the hymn under the dying man's window.

" They call it ", wrote Whytehead to a friend, five days before his death " the ' new hymn of the sick minister.' It is very hard to compress Bishop Ken's fine lines within the same bounds in a rude language. However, it is done, and people seem pleased with it; and it is a comfort to think one has introduced Bishop Ken's beautiful hymn into the Maori's evening worship, and left them this legacy when I could do no more for them."

It has been well said, " A life so short and holy could have had no more beautiful ending."

## The Evangelist's Mistake

Few incidents connected with hymns are so tragic as the following, which occurred when Mr. Moody was first beginning his work as an evangelist in

Chicago. Mr. Moody had been preaching on Bible Characters, and decided to devote the sermons for six successive Sunday nights to the Life of Christ.

On the first Sunday night, October 8, 1871, he preached to the largest congregation he had ever addressed in Chicago on the Trial before Pilate, and having put the claims of Christ before them with intense earnestness, the text being the words " What shall I do with Jesus which is called Christ?" (Matt. 27 : 22), he concluded : " I wish you would take this text home with you, and turn it over in your minds during the week, and next Sabbath we will come to Calvary and the Cross, and we will decide what to do with Jesus of Nazareth!"

Speaking of this in after-years, Mr. Moody called it one of the greatest mistakes of his life.

" For ", he said, " I have never seen that congregation again!"

Having concluded his sermon, he called on Mr. Sankey to sing " To-day the Saviour calls ". Almost prophetically the third verse rang out :

> To-day the Saviour calls;
> For refuge fly;
> The storm of justice falls,
> And death is nigh.

It was the last verse ever sung in that fine hall. For, even as he sang, the singer's voice was drowned by the clang of fire-bells and the rushing of fire-engines in the street. It was the night of the great Fire of Chicago, in which Moody's hall was laid in ashes, and in which it is estimated that over a thousand people perished, some of whom were probably among the evangelist's hearers that evening.

Moody could hardly speak of that night in later years without tears.

"There is one lesson", he used to say, "I learned that night which I have never forgotten, and that is, when I preach, to press Christ upon the people then and there, and try to bring them to a decision on the spot. I would rather have this right hand cut off than give an audience now a week to decide what to do with Jesus!"

## The King of the Cannibal Islands

Little more than a century ago the whole of the South Sea Islands were peopled by the most savage cannibal races. Of these some of the most ferocious were the people of Tonga. In 1821 the natives of Fiji, where many of the inhabitants had become Christian, were terrified by the sight of a Tonga war-canoe rapidly approaching the shore. But its occupants had come not to kill, but—of all things in the world —to buy a Bible!

The people of Tonga had heard of the white man's religion, and wanted to know about it. They had sent a canoe before, which had never been heard of again, and now this second expedition had rowed 250 miles across the open sea in their fragile craft to obtain a copy of the Christian's book, never realizing that it would be entirely useless, since none of them could read! However, a missionary returned with

the party, and so successful was the work in that and
the neighbouring islands that on Whit-Sunday, 1862,
a most remarkable gathering took place.

Under the spreading branches of the banyan-trees
assembled some thousand natives from Tonga, Fiji,
and Samoa, presided over by King George, the old
native monarch who had himself been a cannibal in
his younger days, but was now an earnest follower
of the Lord Jesus Christ, and who had summoned
his people in order to declare his islands Christian,
and to give them a new constitution, exchanging a
heathen for a Christian form of government.

Now they met first of all for divine worship; fore-
most among them all sat King George himself; around
him were old chiefs and warriors who had shared
the perils of many a battle, and, like their sovereign,
had lived in the gross darkness and sins of heathen-
dom. But now all rejoiced together in the gladness
of that great day, their faces radiant with Christian
joy, and love, and hope.

No words could describe the intense feeling manifested when the solemn service began by the whole
multitude singing the words, translated into their own
tongue, of Dr. Watts' great hymn,

> Jesus shall reign where'er the sun
> Doth his successive journeys run.

Who like these, rescued from heathen darkness,
meeting that day for the first time under a Christian
constitution, under a Christian king, and with Christ
Himself reigning in their hearts, could enter into and
realize the full meaning of such words as these:

Blessings abound where'er He reigns,
The prisoner leaps to lose his chains,
The weary find eternal rest,
And all the sons of want are blest?

## *The Stolen Hymns*

Nearly every hymn-book of note contains the hymn beginning " Where high the heavenly temple stands ". Who was the author of this beautiful composition? Most books, in the index, give the name of " Michael Bruce " as the writer, but one book at least gives " Bruce and Logan ", and in those two names is bound up an extraordinary incident in the history of this hymn.

Michael Bruce and John Logan were two young Scotsmen of about the same age, Bruce being born in 1746 and Logan two years later. During the latter years of his short life (he died at the age of twenty-three) Bruce wrote a number of poems, and also several hymns for the use of the singing class at Kinnesswood, the village in which he lived. These compositions were well known to his family and friends, and he eventually copied them out in a quarto manuscript book, hoping that one day he would see them in print.

Immediately after Bruce's death Logan called on his father and asked for the loan of the manuscript book, that he might publish the contents for the benefit of the family, a request which was granted. No publication, however, appeared for three years, and then a book of poems was published under Bruce's name, but the hymns which Bruce's father used to call his son's " Gospel Sonnets " were not included.

As Logan, who was now minister of South Leith, left unanswered all letters and demands for the return of the manuscript book, Mr. Bruce called upon him in person; but the book was not forthcoming, only a few scraps of paper being returned, while Logan excused himself by saying that he feared " the servants had singed fowls with it " !

But eleven years later a second book of poems was published as being the compositions of Logan himself, and with these were included a number of hymns, some of which were immediately recognized both by Bruce and Logan being " Where high the heavenly temple stands ".

There can be little doubt that Logan did thus steal Bruce's hymns, and after the lapse of years endeavour to pass them as his own. It is not a little significant of the man's character that he was finally compelled to resign his pastorate at Leith in order to avoid deposition.


## The Queen's Choice

The hymn, so widely known and loved beginning,

> O happy day that fixed my choice
> On Thee, my Saviour and my God.

and written by Doddridge in the middle of the eighteenth century, is entitled by him " Rejoicing in

Our Covenant Engagement with God." It was, therefore, a fitting thing that Queen Victoria, when one of the Princesses at her Confirmation was about to publicly confess her vows to God, selected this hymn to be sung during the service. The London correspondent, to one of the provincial papers, however, in mentioning this fact, ascribed the authorship of the hymn to Lord Tennyson, and added that he was not worthy of his salary as Poet Laureate if he could not produce anything better than that! It is a pity that the hymn is sometimes spoilt by the addition of a jingling chorus, quite unworthy of association with Doddridge's fine lines.

## The Misty Morning

In the beginning of the year 1883 Messrs. Moody and Sankey conducted a fortnight's mission in the city of Manchester, the scene of their labours being the Free Trade Hall, where each day's work commenced with a meeting at 8 a.m. On one of these mornings the weather was anything but cheering; the sky was dark and the atmosphere cold, while within the huge hall, which was filled from end to end, the mist was so dense that from the platform those at the further end of the hall were scarcely visible.

Gazing on this depressing scene, Mr. Sankey felt that he must sing something of a bright character, In his portfolio was a new hymn, with music, which he had never used up to that time. He decided to introduce this, and in these remarkably appropriate surroundings were sung for the first time the beautiful words, which not only filled the audience with enthusiasm, but became one of Mr. Moody's great favourites :

> When the mists have rolled in splendour
>   From the beauty of the hills,
> And the sunlight falls in gladness
>   On the river and the rills,
> We recall our Father's promise
>   In the rainbow of the spray;
> We shall know each other better
>   When the mists have rolled away.

## From Dying Days

About one hundred years ago there graduated at Oxford a most brilliant scholar of Christ Church College, gaining double first-class honours. At the extraordinary early age of twenty-two, Joseph Anstice was appointed Professor of Classical Literature at King's College, London; six years later the short life reached its end at Torquay.

From his pen, as he entered into the valley of the shadow, came a number of hymns, which are sung to-day by innumerable worshippers, such as " Father by Thy love and power "; " Lord of the harvest, once again "; and " O Lord, how happy should we be ". Some of the words of these well-known hymns are fraught with intense pathos, when we learn the circumstances, as given later by Mrs. Antice, under which they were written. She writes :

" The hymns were all dictated to his wife during the last few weeks of his life, and were composed just at the period of the day (the afternoon) when he felt the oppression of his illness—all his brighter morning hours being given to pupils up to the very day of his death."

How truly pathetic, when we think of the dying man, became such words as those of the closing verse of the third of the above hymns:

> Lord, make these faithless hearts of ours
> Such lessons learn from birds and flowers;
>   Make them from self to cease,
> Leave all things to a Father's will,
> And taste, before Him lying still,
>   E'en in affliction, peace.

## On the Spur of the Moment

In the year 1874 the two American evangelists, Messrs. Moody and Sankey, were entering the train at Glasgow, on their way to begin a campaign of four months at Edinburgh. On the platform Mr. Sankey bought a paper, and, taking his seat, looked through it in the hope of finding some American news. Having glanced through it in vain, he threw the paper down, and only looked at it again just before reaching their destination. Then, in a corner of the paper, he noticed a little piece of poetry, and read for the first time the lines destined to become one of the most famous hymns in the world:

> There were ninety and nine that safely lay
>   In the shelter of the fold;
> But one was out on the hills away,
>   Far off from the gates of gold;
> Away on the mountains wild and bare,
> Away from the tender Shepherd's care.

Immensely impressed by the words, Mr. Sankey proceeded to read them to Mr. Moody, only to find, when he had finished, that Mr. Moody, plunged in thought over a letter, had not heard a single word! However, Mr. Sankey cut out the little poem, and placed it in his music note-book.

At the second day's meeting in Edinburgh Mr. Moody spoke with all his wonted fervour and power on the subject of " The Good Shepherd ". He then called on Dr. Bonar to give a brief address, during which Mr. Moody turned to Mr. Sankey and asked him if he could sing some appropriate solo with which to close the meeting. But Mr. Sankey had nothing suitable in his stock of music.

Suddenly the thought flashed into his mind like a message, " Sing the solo you read in the train." But how could he do this when there was no music for it? Yet he felt that he must sing those words, so placing the newspaper cutting in front of him on his American organ, and lifting up his heart in prayer for help, he essayed the apparently impossible task of composing a tune as he went along for words he had never sung before. Yet as he played, note by note was given to him the tune which everyone to-day knows so well.

At the end of the first verse a fresh difficulty presented itself. Could he accurately repeat the music he had just played? But that too he was enabled to do.

Deeply moved, Mr. Moody came down from the pulpit to Mr. Sankey, and asked him:

"Where did you get that hymn? I never heard the like of it in my life." To which Mr. Sankey replied:

"Why, it is the hymn I read to you in the train yesterday!"

Then, raising his hand, Mr. Moody closed the meeting with the benediction, a benediction which assuredly was not for the great audience only, but which has ever since rested on the hymn so wondrously set to music on the spur of the moment.


## The Preacher's Last Utterance

Dr. Watts' collection of hymns and poems, published under the name of *Horæ Lyricae* in 1705, concluded with the magnificent hymn, beginning,

> Eternal Power, Whose high abode
> Becomes the grandeur of a God,

to which he prefixed the title "God exalted Above All Praise".

There is a pathetically tragic incident which occurred in connection with this hymn. On the morning of Sunday, January 23, 1855, Dr. Joseph Beaumont was announced to preach the Sunday School Anniversary sermons at Waltham Street Chapel, Hull. Although he was suffering considerably from rheumatism, he refused to take any relieving medicine that morning, lest it should interfere with his day's work. The morning was frosty and the streets slippery, but he walked to the chapel leaning on his daughter's arm, and ascended the pulpit stairs at the beginning of the service with apparent ease. The service commenced with Dr. Watts' hymn just referred to, but, instead of reading the first verse, Dr. Beaumont gave out the first two lines of the second, which he pronounced, it is said, with an awful pathos, even his lips quivering as he uttered the solemn words:

> Thee, while the first archangel sings,
> He hides his face behind his wings.

The preacher's emotion was doubtless partially due to the approach of death at that moment, for while the congregation were singing the second of the above lines, and after glancing round as if in search of something, Dr. Beaumont sank down in the place where he stood, whence without any sound, any sign, or any further movement, his soul instantly passed to the presence of that Lord in whose praise he had just uttered these two magnificent lines of Dr. Watts' hymn.

Chapter 10

## SPIRITUAL BLESSING RESULTING FROM HYMNS

### *Saved by the Mother's Hymn*

In connection with the hymn " Jerusalem, my happy home," there is a beautiful story. In a farmhouse in New England, years ago, a mother was accustomed to rock her one little boy to sleep to the accompaniment of her favourite verses:

> Jerusalem, my happy home,
> Name ever dear to me.

Hers had been a sorrowful and laborious life, and at the end of the day the sweet lines brought rest and refreshment to his weary soul. Often, as the boy grew older, and came home in the evening bringing the cows from pasture, he heard her singing,

> Blest seats! through rude and stormy scenes
> I onward press to you.

Later still the mother's voice grew weaker, and more often than any other verse she sang, in feeble tones:

> Why should I shrink at pain or woe,
>     Or feel at death dismay?
> I've Canaan's goodly land in view,
>     And realms of endless day.

Then the mother's voice was hushed for ever, and the father, a hard man, soon made life unbearable for the motherless boy. One night he stole out with his little bundle, including his mother's Bible, and went to a great city, where, falling in with evil companions, he became a dissipated young man. Inheriting his mother's delicate constitution, his excesses told upon his health, until he eventually lay very ill in a common lodging-house. Here he was visited by a city missionary, who became very interested in him; but his ministrations seemed all in vain, and his appeals to him to seek the Saviour appeared to fall on deaf ears. One day, discouraged by his repeated failures, the missionary turned away from the dying man, and, gazing out of the dingy window, he began softly to sing,

> Jerusalem, my happy home,
> Name ever dear to me.

But the first verse was interrupted by a voice from the bed: " Why, that's my mother's hymn!" cried the young fellow, his eyes filled with tears. Back to him came his mother's voice, his mother's love, his mother's prayers. " Oh, that hymn!" he cried, " I have not thought of it for years! How many times it called me home again when I had gone out, angry with my father, and resolved never to go back!"

And now once more the mother's hymn did its work, and called back the erring, rebellious child to the loving arms of the Heavenly Father. Peace and joy became his in Jesus Christ. And when the end came, the good missionary whispered, as he gazed on the peaceful face: " That mother's hymn! It was the means, through Christ, of saving her wandering boy!"

## The Sunday School Child's Wish

A very favourite hymn with children in America, and one which has been translated into several languages, is " I want to be an angel". It had a touching origin. Miss Sidney P. Gill (her curious Christian name being from a Welsh ancestress) was a teacher in the Infant Sunday School in Dr. Joel Parker's church in Philadelphia. She had been giving a lesson to the children on " Angels ", when a lovely little girl in the class exclaimed: " Oh, I want to be an angel!" A few days later the little one was taken ill and died, a circumstance which so impressed Miss Gill that she wrote this hymn, based upon the child's expression of her wish. The first verse runs,

I want to be an angel, and with the angels stand,
A crown upon my forehead, a harp within my hand;
There right before my Saviour, so glorious and so bright,
I'll make the sweetest music, and praise Him day and night.

## The Vanished Tears

The Rev. E. P. Hammond was conducting a children's meeting in America, and was explaining the love of Jesus Christ as shown by his death, when he noticed a girl burst into tears. She remained to the after-meeting, and was pointed to the Saviour in whose love she was soon happy and rejoicing. The next day she brought a letter to Mr. Hammond, from which the following is an extract:

" I think I have found the dear Jesus, and I do not see how I could have rejected Him so long. I think I can sing with the rest of those who have found Him, ' Jesus is mine.' The first time I came to the meetings, I cried; but now I feel like singing all the time."

This last phrase fastened itself in Mr. Hammond's mind, and eventually prompted him to write the well-known hymn, the first verse of which epitomizes the child's letter;

> I feel like singing all the time,
> My tears are wiped away,
> For Jesus is a Friend of mine,
> I'll serve Him every day.

## The Last Verse

One instance of the blessing which has accompanied the beautiful hymn of Dr. Bonar's, " Yet there is room," is full of interest. It was during Messrs. Moody and Sankey's tour in Scotland that a worldly and careless young woman was asked by a friend to accompany her to one of the mission meetings. At first she refused, but, on being further pressed, consented and went. She was not in the least impressed by Mr. Moody's address, which to her seemed to have " nothing in it ", and she wondered that there should be manifested such interest in what was obviously so common-place.

After the address Mr. Sankey sang Dr. Bonar's

composition as a solo, yet even these appealing words left the thoughtless heart of the girl untouched until Mr. Sankey reached the last verse:

Ere night that gate may close, and seal thy doom;
Then the last low long cry—No Room!
No Room! No Room!
Oh, woeful cry—No Room!

The words fell upon the careless soul like the thunder-roll of the Judgement Day. The meeting closed, but the terrible warning of that last verse, and its dreadful refrain, "No Room! No Room!" still rang on in her ears and heart. Nor could she rest until she turned to the Saviour, and, kneeling at His feet, found pardon and peace through His redeeming Blood.

## Far Off from the Gates of Gold

A lady who had been much interested in the work of the two evangelists, Messrs Moody and Sankey, took some of their hymn-books with her on a visit to Paris, with a view to their distribution, and on the evening of her arrival placed one on the table in the reading-room of her hotel.

After dinner a young Englishman, just come over to Paris for a fortnight's dissipation, caught sight of the book among the papers. He was familiar with the names of Moody and Sankey, since his sister, an earnest Christian, had worked with them, and often urged him, but in vain, to attend their meetings. Carelessly he opened the book, and his eye fell on the two lines,

> But one was out on the hills away,
> Far off from the gates of gold.

" I suppose Mary would say that's me ", he said to himself, and, tossing the book aside, went out to attend the Opera. But he failed in all attempts to put those words out of his mind. Even in the Opera House, amid all the beautiful music and the gaiety of his surroundings, he seemed to hear over and over again the refrain,

> But one was out on the hills away,
> Far off from the gates of gold.

He was glad to get back to his hotel and retire to bed, but with his first conscious moment the next morning the words returned as before, until at the end of a few days he was miserable.

At last it occurred to him to find the book again, and see what the rest of the hymn might be. The book was easily found on the reading-room table, but being unfamiliar with the opening words, it took him some time to find the hymn. At length he discovered it, and began to read,

> There were ninety and nine that safely lay
> In the shelter of the fold.

" Ah! that's Mary," he said to himself; " she is safe in the fold."

179

But one was out on the hills away,
Far off from the gates of gold.

" And that's me ", he murmured. It was no longer " Mary would say "; he himself knew it now. A day or two afterwards, falling ill, he was attended by a doctor, also staying in the hotel, who was himself an earnest Christian. To him the young man opened his heart, and by the doctor's help he was led to yield himself to the Good Shepherd who, in this strange way, had used the hymn to bring home wandering sheep.

## Outside the Door

Among the many souls blessed through the hymn known best by its refrain, " Take me as I am," was that of an infidel, in whom, during Messrs. Moody and Sankey's campaign in Plymouth, Professor Drummond, who was working with them, was much interested. The man lived twenty miles out of Plymouth, but had been to some of the services, and Drummond endeavoured to win him for Christ, even visiting him in his home, but to no purpose.

Towards the close of the campaign the man came to Plymouth again, but on reaching the building in which the meetings were held he found the place full and the door closed. It was there, outside the building, that his conversion to God took place, and the means of it was the singing by the choir of " Take me as I am," which reached not only his ears but

180

his heart, and led him into the Kingdom as he stood outside the door.

## The Hymn that Changed the Sermon

Ira D. Sankey composed the music to Elizabeth Clephane's delightful hymn "Beneath the Cross of Jesus I fain would take my stand," in the house of the late Dr. Barnardo, so well known for his work among outcast children. The following morning, at eight o'clock, the usual Mission Service was held in the Bow Road Hall in East London, the preacher on that occasion being Canon Hay Aitken, the well-known missioner, who, though over eighty years of age, still conducted parochial missions. Mr. Moody, the usual speaker, was engaged elsewhere on that morning.

It was a glorious morning, and a very large congregation was present, despite the early hour. It was arranged that Mr. Sankey should sing a solo before the sermon, and he elected to sing " Beneath the Cross of Jesus," to the music composed the previous day. The effect was tremendous.

When the solo was finished, Mr. Aitken, his eyes filled with tears, told the deeply moved audience that he had intended to speak that morning on the subject of Christian work, but the new hymn had made such an impression not only on himself, but obviously upon his hearers, that he had decided to preach upon " The Cross of Jesus ". The sermon that followed was most powerful, and was used of God in that early morning hour to bring many to the Saviour.

## The Last Refrain

Mr. Lewis Hartsough's favourite hymn, " I Hear Thy welcome Voice," of which he wrote both words and music, was first published in an American monthly magazine, called *Guide to Holiness*. A copy was sent to Mr. Sankey, who was then with Mr. Moody in England, and he at once included it in his *Sacred Songs and Solos*, finding it most useful in their mission work. Not long after its publication it was being used in a church in Washington as an invitation hymn, the large congregation standing and singing it while those who desired to seek the Saviour were invited to come forward and kneel at the altar rails.

It chanced that a merchant of the city, who had not entered a church for twenty years, was passing the building, and, hearing the singing, stopped to listen. As verse after verse was sung, the impression made upon him was so deep that he went into the church, and, passing up the aisle, joined the penitents at the rails. His conversion to God was very real and true, and the hymn that had been the means of bringing him to the Saviour naturally became his favourite from that hour; he sang it wherever he went.

About a fortnight later, on a wintry morning, he left home for business as usual, and his wife, who stood for a moment at the door where he had wished her good-bye, heard him begin to sing his favourite refrain as he passed into the street :

> I am coming, Lord,
>   Coming now to Thee;
> Wash me, cleanse me in the Blood
>   That flowed on Calvary.

After listening for a moment, she closed the door, and re-entered the room. A few minutes later the door-bell rang, and she herself went to open it. There stood without a little group of men bearing her husband's dead body. Only a few yards down the street he had slipped upon the frozen pavement, and had been killed on the spot.

The refrain of the hymn which had led him to the feet of the Saviour on earth were the last words on his lips as he passed to the Saviour's Presence in Paradise:

> I am coming, Lord,
> Coming now to Thee.

## Converted by a Hymn

In 1912, when I was compiling *The Church Mission Hymn Book*, in collaboration with Canon A. E. Barnes-Lawrence, I wished to set one of my own hymns to a tune by Mr. G. B. Blanchard, organist of a Wesleyan Church in Hull, and I therefore applied to Mr. Blanchard for permission.

No answer was received for a fortnight, and then Mr. Blanchard replied, relating the following interesting incident. He said that his tune had been specially written for a children's hymn from his own pen, and as he considered the tune was by wide use wedded to that hymn, he did not feel at all disposed to allow it to be set to another. But before he finally decided he thought he would try the effect of the suggested hymn, sung to his own tune, as a solo at a Sunday

183

Evening Mission Service with which he was connected. "During the singing of the solo," wrote Mr. Blanchard, "a person in the audience yielded to the Saviour. I cannot now refuse you the use of my tune." Readers of these pages may be interested, and perhaps some may be helped, by the printing of the hymn in full.

Hear the Voice of Jesus calling, soft and clear—
For the Lord of Life and Glory standeth here:
" Come to Me, O souls distressed, by sin undone,
For I love you, and would save you every one."

Now the wounded Feet are drawing to thy side;
Shall they pass beyond and leave thee, or abide?
Wilt thou bid thy loving Saviour turn away?—
Or within thy heart to enter and to stay?

See the piercèd Hands outstretching now to thee
Hands for love of thee outstretched on Calvary,
Hands of Him Who all thy debt of sin hath paid,
Hands that wait to feel thine own within them laid.

Look, the thorn-crowned Head is bending over thee,
And the patient Eyes are watching tenderly—
Watching for thy heart to yield, thy lips to say—
" Jesus, Master, take me, save me here to-day."

And the Saviour's Heart is yearning, in its love,
Here to save thee, and to keep thee—then, above,
There to welcome thee, and set thee on His throne;
Wilt thou give thyself to Jesus for his own?

## In the Church Aisle

The Rev. Canon Hay Aitken, the famous missioner, tells the story of a young lady, fashionable and worldly, who was persuaded to attend one of the services at a mission which he was conducting in the

West End of London. Apparently the preacher's earnest pleading and appeals did not move her in the least, and as soon as the sermon was ended she rose to leave the church before the after-meeting. But the church was full and the aisle crowded with people, so that her progress towards the door was very slow, and as she moved along she became very interested in the appealing hymn, "Lord, I hear of showers of blessing," with its constant refrain, "Even me! Even me!" Strangely enough, the hymn was new to her, and she followed the lines in her own book which was in her hand, until, just as she was approaching the church door, the choir reached the last verse of the hymn :

> Pass me not! Thy lost one bringing,
> Bind my heart, O Lord, to Thee!
> While the streams of life are springing,
> Blessing others, O bless me! Even me!

As the words were sung, the thought suddenly flashed into her mind, "I am the lost one!" All along her homeward way the words rang on in her heart, "Pass me not! Thy lost one bringing." Presently she was alone in her bedroom, lying on her bed, sobbing out from the depths of her soul the pleading prayer, "Pass me not! Thy lost one bringing." Then came the remembrance of the Saviour's words that He, "came to seek and to save that which was lost", and ere she slept that night her soul had found rest in that Saviour's love, and her new life in Christ begun.

# INDEX OF HYMNS

# INDEX OF AUTHORS